Sew Any Patch Pocket

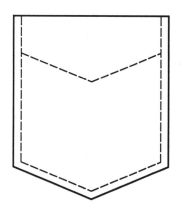

Published by
Chilton Book Company
Radnor, Pennsylvania 19089

ISBN 0-932086-25-X

Library of Congress Catalog
Card Number 91-068104

Printed in the United States of America

Designer: Martha Vercoutere
Illustrator: Pamela S. Poole
Fashion Art: Bracey Plaeger
Seamstress: Pat Whittemore
Photographer: Lee Lindeman
Production Director: Cate Keller
Editor: Robbie Fanning

For help with pocket tips, thanks to:

Carol Ahles
Clotilde
Jackie Dodson
Miss Adeline Giuntini
Margaret Komives
Liz Mann
Mr. Michael
Nancy Nix-Rice
Shirley Smith
Jane Whiteley
Pat Whittemore
Nancy Zieman

Sew Any
Patch Pocket

Claire B. Shaeffer

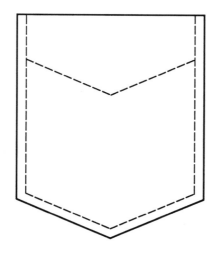

Chilton Book Company
Radnor, Pennsylvania

Table of Contents

Letter From the Publisher .....*vi*

How to Use This Book ....*vi*

Preface .... *vii*

Introduction......................... *vii*

Part I: The Pockets

1. Unlined Patch Pockets 1

Basic Unlined Pocket 2
Kangaroo Pocket 4
Man's Shirt Pocket 5
Jeans Pocket 7
Unlined Pocket With Tucked Hem 8
Unlined Pocket With Band 10
Gathered Pocket With Band 12
Faced Edges 13
Unlined Pocket With Ribbon Facing 14
Decorative Faced Opening 15
Elasticized Opening 17
Gathered Pouch 19

2. Lined Patch Pockets 20

Basic Lined Pocket 21
Easy Lined Pocket 23
Couture Lined Pocket 24
Flat-Lined Pocket 26
Decorative Edge-to-Edge Lining 27
Utilitarian Edge-to-Edge Lining 28
Utilitarian Edge-to-Edge Lining—Hook
    Method 29
One-Piece Self-Lined Pockets 30
Self-Lined Pocket With Bound Edge 32
Fake Inside-Stitched Pocket 34
Magic-Lined Patch Pocket 35
Round Pocket With Button 37

3. Novelty Pockets 38

Inside-Stitched Pocket 39
Square Inside-Stitched Pocket 42
Pockets With Cuffs 43
Lined Pocket With Cut-on Cuff 43
Unlined Pocket With Cut-on Cuff 45
Unlined Pocket With One-Piece Cuff 47
Pockets With Tucks 49
Pocket With Pintucks 50
Easy Tucked Pocket 51
Pocket With Overlapping Tucks 53
Pocket With Cross Tucks 54
Tucked Stripes 56
Reverse Tucks 56
Pocket With Notched Tucks 57
Pleated Pockets 59
Pocket With Inverted Pleat 61
Pocket With Inverted Pleat
    (Separate Underlay) 63
Pocket With Box Pleat 64
Pleated Pocket With Band 67
Banded Pocket With Flared Pleat 68
Pleated Pocket With Shaped Band 70
Pleated Pocket With Flap 70

Bellows Pockets 71
Unlined One-Piece Bellows Pocket 72
Bellows Pocket With Separate
    Gusset 75
Bellows Pocket With Flap 78
Saddle Bag Pockets 79
Saddle Bag With Flap 79
Pocket Patches 82
Easy Lined Patch 82
Pocket Patch With Bound Edges 84

4. *Flaps* 85

Separate Flaps 86
Flap Applications 88
  All-purpose Application 88
  Application for Lightweight Fabrics 90
  Couture Application 90

Part II: *General Directions for Patch Pockets*

Pocket Location and Placement 92

  The Perfect Location 92
  Marking Pocket Placement 93

Interfacings 94
  How to Interface Pockets 94
    Fusible Interfacings 94
    Sew-in Interfacings 95
    Quick-and-Easy Application 95
    Designer Application 95
    Trenched Application 96
  How to Interface Hems 97

Reinforced Openings 97
Underlining Pockets 98
Finishes for Pocket Openings 99
  Traditional Hems 99
  Narrow Topstitched Hems 102
  Bindings 102

Setting the Pocket 102
  General Directions for Applying Patch
    Pockets 103
  Pressing Techniques 105
    Shaping the Pocket 106
  Reinforcing the Garment Under the
    Pocket 106

Hints for Special Fabrics 107
  Plaids 107
  Sweater Knits 108

Appendices ....

Designer's Worksheet 109
Three Pocket Patterns 110
Sources 113
Publications 113
Glossary 114
Bibliography 115
Index 116

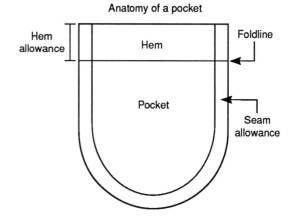

Anatomy of a pocket

Hem allowance · Hem · Foldline · Pocket · Seam allowance

Letter from the Publisher

I am walking down the ramp in the Palm Springs airport behind a line of passengers. Do I notice the mountains, dramatic against the desert? the distinctive style of architecture? even the 104° blast of heat?

No, I notice none of the above, because I have been possessed: I notice only the asymmetric cant of back jeans pockets. Once you learn that they are not parallel and not symmetrical, you, too, will be possessed. Never again will you stand in line anywhere without staring at western backsides and thinking, "I'll be hornswaggled—they are asymmetric!"

Call it Pocket Possession and blame it on Claire.

In the beginning, my husband wanted me to make pockets all over a leather vest. I couldn't find the information I needed to design and sew the pockets, so I asked Claire to write a 128-page book. Simple task, no?

But when you begin to examine pockets, there are hundreds of kinds. We've included 50 in this book—and that's only patch pockets!

Eventually, Claire wrote 372 pages of manuscript, all on pockets and all good material. So we're publishing two books, one on patch pockets and one on inset pockets (see the last page).

Pockets, after all, are tiny mirrors of almost all sewing techniques. You can practice pattern design, seam and hem finishing, interfacing, lining, edgestitching and topstitching, and decorative techniques.

You can jazz up ready-to-wear by removing, decorating, and replacing pockets.

You can have fun designing unique clothing without spending hours on construction.

And most of all, you will look at the world of walking pockets with new (obsessed) eyes.

Robbie Fanning
Menlo Park, CA

How to Use This Book

1. Choose a pocket to make. You may see something in ready-to-wear or in a magazine that attracts your eye. Photocopy the Designer's Worksheet on page 109 and play with possible designs.

2. Analyze your pocket: Is it lined or unlined? Does it have flaps? Does it have a novelty feature like an unusual shape or a special treatment of patterned fabric? Look at the illustrations in this book. Find the closest pocket to your idea and read its Pattern Development and Sewing Notes.

3. Make a sample. You'll be glad you took the extra time and you'll have a reference for the next time you make that pocket. But please note: The directions for your pocket assume you have already read the General Directions in Part II. If you need to refresh your memory when your pocket directions say, "Interface as needed" or "Set the pocket," read the General Directions.

4. Share what you've learned. Show others your pocket samples. Teach someone else. Pockets are an easy, fast way to practice sewing skills.

Preface

This book is one of my dreams come true. It isn't an ordinary sewing book; it's actually a design-and-sew book. All of the designs are for patch pockets, but many of the individual elements of each design can be applied to any type garment or garment section.

I adore pockets—all sizes, all shapes, all types. Naturally, all my favorite garments have pockets and I'm always looking for better construction techniques and new pocket designs on the latest high-fashion designs.

I like pockets for all the same reasons you like them. They are wonderful receptacles for little treasures, like a handkerchief or lipstick, and big necessities, like keys, rain hat, gloves, or notepad and pen. They keep my hands warm and cozy when the weather's cold and rainy, and they even hide my hands when I don't know what else to do with them.

I particularly like to teach pocketmaking because pockets are like keys. They are small, easy to handle, and wait patiently to open many exciting doors for you. Some are unusual, some are plain and ordinary, some open many different doors, and several open the same door. They will lead you to more professional results, to unlock the mysteries of design, and to unleash your creative talents.

In this book, instead of including a bunch of pocket patterns with specific directions how to sew each one, I show you how to develop *any* pocket pattern so that you can create similar, but original, designs of your own. Sometimes, when you're anxious to make a pocket in a hurry, you'll be annoyed with my detailed instructions; but when your creative juices start to flow and you want something fabulously different, you'll be glad that I led you through the patternmaking process one step at a time. And if an occasional pocket doesn't meet your standards, you can simply make another one— it won't take much fabric.

I encourage my students to make lots of samples. After all, most have a box of fabric scraps—I have several—which are too precious to discard. They're perfect for pocket samples. Experiment and practice. Don't worry at the beginning about the end results. Just sew and sew and sew until your fingers dance like a pianist playing Chopin.

Save your best pockets and even some of the not-so-good ones in a notebook or box so you can appreciate your progress. And if you have time between pockets and other projects, write me in care of Open Chain Publishing, Inc., send me pictures, and tell me about your successes and failures.

Claire Shaeffer
Palm Springs, CA

Introduction

Hints for Patch Pockets

Also known as applied pockets, most patch pockets are made by sewing a piece of fabric to the outside of the garment so one edge—usually the top—is left open for the hand. They are popular with both sexes, all age groups, and used on every type of garment. Adding a patch pocket to a basic silhouette is one of the easiest ways to create an original design. This was particularly popular during the '70s, when the only difference between many designs was the surface elements—pockets, flaps, welts, tabs, and braids.

Patch pockets are easy to make, but if they aren't perfect, they'll make the garment look homemade.

When designing pockets, study current trends and examine the pockets on ready-made garments, as well as photographs in catalogs and magazines. You'll find an endless variety—all shapes and sizes, plain or trimmed—in all fabrications.

Pockets can be used singly, in pairs, or in multiples, but usually single pockets are easier to place attractively than pairs.

Generally, the pocket shape echoes other garment details. On designs with round collars, cuffs, or yokes, pockets with rounded corners are the safest choice, but square pockets with round flaps are sometimes used.

Although the pocket size should be appropriate for the size of the wearer and/or the garment, the pocket size is also influenced by the garment style, the pocket location, and current fashion trends. Don't forget that patch pockets appear larger than inset pockets.

Decorative pockets can be any size, but functional pockets should be 1" to 2" wider than the hand's width. Pockets on the upper part of the garment are usually smaller than those on the lower section or skirt. When located at the hipline, pockets should be large enough to put your hand into them, but if they're too large, they'll appear to add unwanted pounds.

Hint: Use fabric scraps to cut a "design pocket" without any seam or hem allowances. Pin it in place on the almost-finished garment and adjust until the desired effect is achieved; then make a real pocket and apply it to the garment. This tip comes from Mr. Michael, the tailor at Hardy Amies (Dressmaker to the Queen of England).

Let the crispness or softness of the fabric hand influence the pocket design. Use crisp fabrics for tailored and geometric pockets and soft fabrics for pretty curved or draped pockets.

When designing the pocket, consider the overall garment style. On traditional, tailored designs, an unmatched pair—a round pocket on one side and a square one on the other—will look ridiculous; on a casual, cotton jacket, it can be an interesting design detail.

When designing children's wear, it's also reassuring to know that they don't "outgrow" patch pockets as quickly as other types. It's obvious when welt pockets are too high but a too-high patch is not as noticeable.

Hint: Don't overlook heirloom stitching expert Carol Ahles' Band-aid Pocket—a pocket used to trim a wounded garment. One day when Carol's daughter Emily was in kindergarten, she inadvertently clipped the fabric on her favorite dress—a beautiful dusty pink Bishop with hand-smocked hearts around the neckline and sleeves. Clever Carol made a pocket with the heart motifs at the opening and applied it over the hole. Carol confesses that the pocket was more centered than usual, but it wasn't noticeable. Best of all, Emily enjoyed the dress two more years.

Standards for Patch Pockets

1. Applied pockets should be constructed and applied appropriately for the garment design, quality, and use, as well as the fabric pattern, bulk, weight, transparency, and hand.

2. Pocket corners should be reinforced appropriately for the pocket use.

3. No thread ends or raw edges should be visible.

4. Seam and hem allowances should be inconspicuous and bulk-free.

5. Raw edges should not peek out at the corners.

6. Seamlines should be hidden, unless designed otherwise.

7. Pockets should maintain their shape and be interfaced as needed.

8. Pockets should lie smooth without pulling, twisting, or sagging when the garment is worn.

9. The pocket opening or pocket mouth should not stretch out of shape when the pocket is used.

10. Pockets and flaps should be cut precisely on the indicated grain.

11. Straight edges should be straight.

12. Curved corners and edges should be smoothly rounded, flat, and symmetrical.

13. Square corners should have well-formed angles and be flat and symmetrical.

14. Pockets should be symmetrical unless designed otherwise.

15. Pockets should match the fabric pattern, grain, and nap of the garment section unless designed otherwise. If the entire pocket cannot be matched to the fabric pattern, it should match at the edge toward the center or at the bottom.

16. Topstitching should be appropriate for the design and fabric. It should be evenly stitched from the edges; the length should be appropriate for the fabric, and all stitches should be the same length.

17. Functional pockets should be located and designed for use. The pocket opening should be large enough for the hand to be inserted easily, and the pocket depth should be appropriate for the wearer so the hand can reach the bottom.

18. On lined pockets, the lining should not be visible and the turning point should be inconspicuous from the right side of the garment.

19. Paired pockets should be identical in size, shape, and placement. They should be equidistant, or look equidistant, from the garment center and be located at the same height.

20. Pockets with trims should be set neatly and appropriately for the design, location, use, and fabric.

21. Interfacings, underlinings, and linings should have the same care requirements as the garment.

22. The garment should be reinforced under the pocket mouth of functional pockets.

General Directions for Making a Patch Pocket Pattern

Directions for making specific patch pocket patterns are found in the following chapters. These directions apply to any pocket.

1. Make a rough sketch or copy a photograph in your file of pocket ideas. See the Designer's Worksheet on page 109. Photocopy it and play with possible designs.

2. Draw the pocket on the garment pattern. Locate it and draw it exactly like it will look on the finished garment. It should be the same size, shape, and location.

> **Hint:** *Don't worry about seam and hem allowances at this time. If the pocket has a flap or one part laps over another, draw the section you'll see with a solid line and the concealed section with a broken line or different color pencil.*

3. If you're not making a test garment (toile), try on the paper pattern to see if the pocket size, shape, and location are appropriate. Or compare the pocket placement and size to similar designs in your wardrobe or current fashions.

> **Hint:** *You don't have to make a final decision now, but it's always easier to apply pockets before the garment is assembled.*

4. Trace the pocket onto pattern paper.

> **Hint:** *I use physician's examining paper, available from medical supply houses (see the Yellow Pages), but wax paper, butcher paper, and pattern cloth are also good choices. If you can't see through the pattern paper, place the original pattern on top and trace with a stiletto tracing wheel.*

5. If the pocket has pleats, darts, or gathers, add them to the basic shape.

6. Decide whether the pocket will be lined or unlined and how the opening will be finished. Add the appropriate seam or hem allowance.

7. Add seam allowances to the remaining edges.

8. Indicate the grainline. Generally, the grainline duplicates the grainline on the garment, but for design interest, the grainline can be anyway you like.

> **Hint:** *To make a bias grainline, fold an envelope diagonally so the end matches one long side. Align the side of the envelope with the grainline on the pattern. Draw the new grainline at the diagonal fold.*

To draw the grainline at right angles, carefully align one short edge of the envelope with the grainline on the pattern. Draw the new grainline at the top of the envelope.

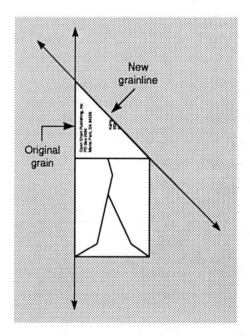

Part I: The Pockets

1. Unlined Patch Pockets

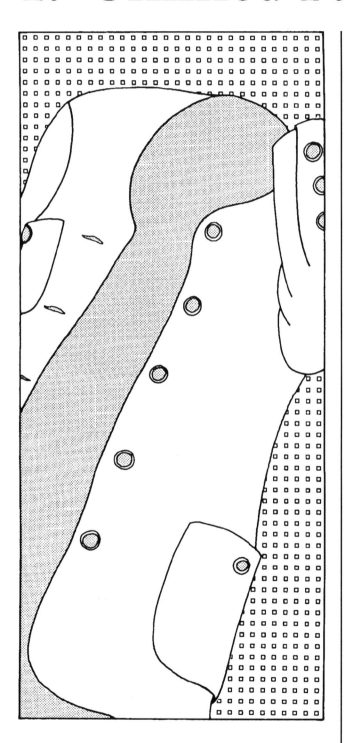

Basic unlined pockets can run the gamut from small to large, functional to decorative. They can be located almost anywhere on a variety of garments—ladies' blouses, skirts, sportswear, and children's designs—and made in fabrics ranging from very lightweight sheers to medium-weight wools.

Unlined pockets are most attractive when made of firmly woven fabrics and stable knits. They are frequently used on casual designs, children's garments, jeans, and shirts.

Since you must decide how you will apply an unlined pocket before you cut the pattern, please read Part II: General Directions for Pockets, especially from page 102 on.

Basic Unlined Pocket

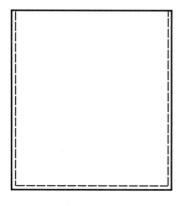

Design Analysis:

Generally applied by machine with topstitching, edgestitching, or inside stitching (page 39), basic pockets can be any shape—triangular, square, or novelty; but most are small- to medium-sized rectangles which are most attractive when the depth is greater than the width. The pocket bottom can be squared-off, curved, or pointed.

The pocket opening is usually finished with an inconspicuous 1"- to 1-1/2"-wide self-fabric hem, but it can be finished with a narrow, topstitched hem.

Pattern Development:

1. Outline the finished pocket. Add a 1-1/4" to 1-1/2" hem allowance at the top and 5/8" seam allowances to the sides and bottom.

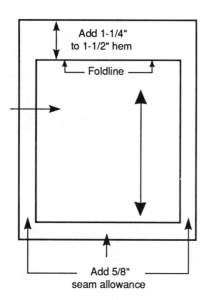

Add 1-1/4" to 1-1/2" hem

Foldline

Add 5/8" seam allowance

2. Indicate the grainline and foldline. It usually duplicates the grain on the garment or is placed at right angles to the pocket opening, but the grainline can be parallel to the foldline or the pocket can be cut on the bias for a novelty effect.

3. Cut out the pocket pattern.

Hints: When the pocket is not rectangular or when the opening is on a slant, fold the hem in place before cutting so the hem will fit the pocket. (See page 99.)

On small pockets with rounded corners, Nancy Nix-Rice recommends reshaping the curve to an angle which is easier to press under and it looks more fashionable. If the fabric is a plaid, cut the pocket on the bias so the corners will be on grain. Don't forget to stablize the pocket with a fusible interfacing.

Sewing Notes:

1. Cut one pocket from the fashion fabric. Mark each end of the pocket foldline with short clips.

Cut an interfacing if needed. (See page 94.)

Hint: Pockets made from crisp, firmly woven fabrics or transparent fabrics are least likely to need interfacings. Pockets made from knits, wools, soft, or flimsy materials are most likely to need them.

2. Interface the pocket or stay the pocket opening as needed. (See How to Interface on page 94.)

3. Finish the raw edge of the hem (see Traditional Hems on page 99):

On lightweight cottons, polyesters, and silks, clean finish the edge.

On bulky or heavy fabrics, finish the edge with a multi-stitch zigzag, regular zigzag, serging, or seam tape.

4. Decide how you plan to sew the pocket to the garment—topstitching, edgestitching, or invisible handstitching. Then finish the hem allowance ends on each side of the pocket. If the pocket has rounded corners, crimp or ease baste (see page 114) the curved sections 1/4" from the edge.

Here are three easy finishes for hem allowances:

Dressmaker Method: This finish is appropriate when the pocket will be edgestitched in place. It encloses the seam allowances at the pocket opening; however, the edge of the pocket hem may show if the stitching isn't close to the pocket edges. Fold the pocket at the foldline, right sides together. Stitch each end of the hem just inside the seamline. Trim to the bottom of the hem allowance. Turn the hem right side out and press.

Dressmaker
Method

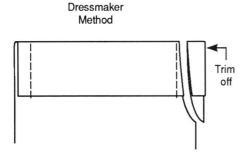

Trim
off

Shirt Method: With this finish, the sides are smooth and look terrific when the pocket is edgestitched or topstitched, but the seam ends at the pocket opening may show unless you hide them carefully. Fold the pocket at the foldline, wrong sides together. Baste guideline just inside the seamline, and press the seam allowances to the wrong side. Fold the seam allowance corners at the top of the pocket, in between the seam allowance and pocket hem.

Shirt
Method

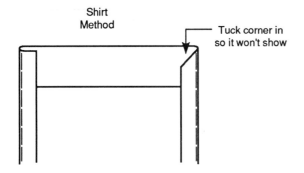

Tuck corner in
so it won't show

Designer Method: With this finish, both the sides and opening are smooth. On the raw edge at the top of the pocket, measure and mark 7/8" from each side. Press the pocket seam allowances under 5/8"—do not press the seam allowances on the pocket hem. Wrong sides together, press the opening. Tuck under the ends of the pocket hem, tapering to the marked points, and press. Clip out the excess bulk at the fold.

Designer
Method

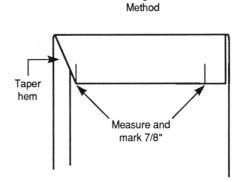

Taper
hem

Measure and
mark 7/8"

5. Stitch around the pocket just inside the seamline. If the fabric is bulky, miter any corners.

Hint: Serger owners may prefer this super idea from Nancy Nix-Rice, a former product manager for baby lock. Fold the hem at the top to the right side. Then serge around the pocket with the serger needle right on the seamline. This not only reduces the seam bulk but it also marks the seamline itself. Turn right-side-out. The remaining 1/4" seam allowance presses under "like a dream."

6. Wrong side up, press the seam allowances to the wrong side so the stitched line is barely visible.

For perfect pockets, press over a cardboard template the size and shape of the finished pocket. Insert it between the pocket and seam allowances.

On squared or chevron pockets, press the bottom edge first; then press the sides. (See Step 2 on page 105.)

On curved pockets, pull up the bobbin thread and adjust the gathers in the curved sections so they fit smoothly on the wrong side of the pocket.

Hint: *Some of my students like the Pocket Former—a gadget that holds the fabric in place for you when you're pressing curves. Since each corner on this little gadget has a different curve, be sure to press all pocket corners over the same curve. I don't particularly like the Pocket Former, but I do like the little holder and frequently use it with my cardboard templates.*

Hint: *Pat Whittemore, who stitched samples of all the pockets, uses freezer paper as a template. She cuts it out the finished size, cuts a small X in the center top to make removal easier, and irons the shiny side of the paper against the wrong side of the pocket. She does the same for the hem allowance, but separately, so she can peel it up easily. After pressing in the seam allowance over the paper, Pat peels up the freezer paper with an orange peeler. See page 104 for another way to use freezer paper.*

7. When making pocket pairs, compare them before proceeding to be sure they're identical.

8. Trim and notch the seam allowances so the seam allowance will lie flat.

9. Topstitch and/or edgestitch the upper edge if appropriate for the garment design.

10. Baste the pocket in place using a glue stick, fusible web, or water-soluble thread.

11. Here are two ways to set the pocket to the garment:

Set the pocket to the garment by hand or machine.

For functional pockets, edgestitch near the fold and/or topstitch 1/4" away. Begin and end with a spottack. Pull all threads to the underside, knot, and trim.

Hint: *To reduce the collection of dirt and lint, topstitch the pocket again so the seam allowances are enclosed.*

For frequently used pockets, rough-and-tumble garments, or children's designs, reinforce the corners of the pocket with a simple backstitch, short horizontal stitch at the ends, triangle, rectangle, or bartack (see page 105).

Secure it invisibly with a hand stitch if the pocket won't be used a lot.

Hint: *With the garment right side up, I baste around the pocket 1/4" from the edge. Then, with the garment wrong side up, I place a running stitch or catchstitch about 1/8" away. I don't like a slipstitch. It's too time consuming, and since it always shows, it makes the pocket look homemade. Reinforce the corner from the wrong side with a catchstitch.*

Variation: Kangaroo Pocket

A variation of the Basic Unlined Pocket, the Kangaroo Pocket is frequently found on sweat shirts. It is symmetrical and centered, with six sides and two openings. The Kangaroo Pocket is secured at the top and bottom by topstitching or by a seam and is open at the sides like a pouch. The edges are generally finished by turning the hem allowances under and topstitching 1/4" and 1/2" from the edge, but they can also be bound with ribbing or binding.

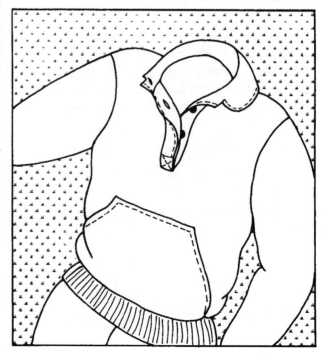

Man's Shirt Pocket

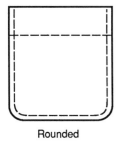

Rounded

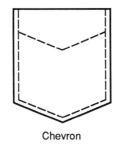

Chevron

Design Analysis:

The Man's Shirt Pocket is probably the most popular pocket in use. At first glance, all shirt pockets look alike. But when I examined several closely, I found differences in the size of pockets, depth of the hem, shape of the pocket and hem, and relationship of the hem shape to the bottom of the pocket.

You can see in the illustrations below, which I copied from expensive menswear, that there are no rules cast in concrete. Straight hems are rarely used on expensive dress shirts; but they are used on good quality sport shirts, especially under flaps or when the pocket buttons to the shirt. Here are some variations:

1. 1-1/8" straight hem with rounded corners; 2. 1-3/4" chevron hem with rounded corners; 3. 1-5/8" chevron hem with 7/8" bottom chevron; 4. 1-1/2" chevron hem with 1-3/4" bottom chevron.

Usually located on the left side of the shirt, most pockets are rectangular and measure about 4-1/2" by 5-1/4". Generally, the better all-cotton, English shirts have rounded corners at the bottom, while sport shirts have a chevron.

Hint: If you're a pocket lover and a non-shirtmaker, you'll appreciate author Jackie Dodson's idea. Her husband Chuck really likes pockets—two are always better than one—so she shortens the sleeves on long-sleeved shirts and uses the left-over sleeve bottoms to make extra pockets.

Pattern Development:

1. Draw a rectangle 4-1/2" by 5-1/4". Outline the finished pocket within the rectangle.

Hints: *An easy way to design this pocket is to fold the tracing paper lengthwise and draw only one half.*

To draw rounded corners, use a cardboard circle with a 2" diameter. Move it into the corner until it touches the seamlines at the side and bottom. If you don't like the way the curve looks, try a larger circle. Also see page 112.

If you prefer a chevron, make it 3/8" to 1" deep at the center. Also see page 111.

2. Draw the finished hem on the pocket. It is usually straight on sport shirts and shaped with a chevron on dress shirts.

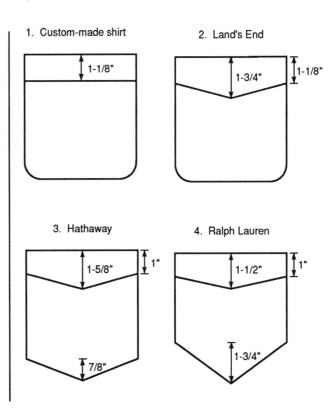

1. Custom-made shirt — 1-1/8"

2. Land's End — 1-3/4", 1-1/8"

3. Hathaway — 1-5/8", 1", 7/8"

4. Ralph Lauren — 1-1/2", 1", 1-3/4"

3. Fold the tracing paper forward at the pocket foldline and trace the hem. Add a 1/4" allowance at the edge of the hem for edge finishing. Add 1/4" seam allowances to the pocket sides and bottom.

4. Indicate the grainline. It is usually at right angles to the opening, but on one Hathaway shirt I saw, it was parallel to the foldline and the selvage was used to finish the hem. On novelty sport and western shirts, the pocket is sometimes cut on the bias.

Sewing Notes:

1. Cut one pocket—most shirts have only one on the left side. Mark each end of the pocket foldline with short clips.

2. Press the hem to the wrong side of the pocket. Fold the raw edge under, forming a small tuck at the point of the chevron. Press the tuck neatly. Edgestitch the hem in place. Press.

Hint: On some expensive English-made dress shirts, the hems are folded to the right side. The right-side-out hem can only be used on fabrics which look the same on both sides or which have an attractive reverse side.

3. If the pocket buttons to the shirt, mark the buttonhole location on the pocket. Most are located at the center of the hem parallel to the grainline. Occasionally, the buttonhole is parallel to the opening.

Hint: Locate the buttonhole so that when the pocket is buttoned, the edge of the button will be at least 1/8" from the pocket foldline. I use this formula—half the button diameter plus 1/8"—when measuring.

4. Press the seam allowances to the wrong side.

On a rectangular or chevron pocket, press the bottom, then the sides. The seam allowance at the point will form a small tuck. Press it down neatly. For a perfect chevron, stitch the bottom of the pocket almost-but-not-quite on the seamline before pressing. Then, wrong side up, press the chevron under, using the stitched line as a guide.

On a pocket with rounded corners, crimp the curved sections 3/8" from the edge before pressing and press over a cardboard template.

Tuck the upper corners in between the seam and hem allowances. Press.

5. Right sides up, place the pocket on the shirt front so it is 5-3/4" – 6" below the neckline at the center front and about 2-1/4" from the center front. Baste.

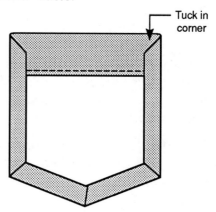

Tuck in corner

Hints: If the shirt has only one pocket, it's located on the left front for right-handed wearers. If the wearer is left-handed, this position would be awkward, but pockets on both sides usually look better than one on the right side.

6. Edgestitch the pocket in place. Reinforce the pockets with a triangle at the beginning and end (see page 105). Pull all threads to the underside, knot, and trim.

7. If the pocket has a pencil slot, stitch it 1" wide.

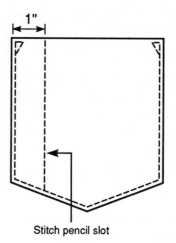

1"

Stitch pencil slot

8. Press.

Jeans Pocket

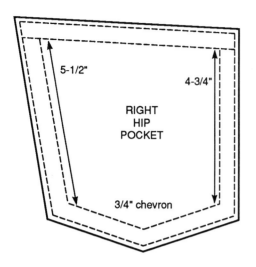

5-1/2"

4-3/4"

RIGHT
HIP
POCKET

3/4" chevron

Design Analysis:

The back pockets on jeans are usually asymmetrical and the pocket top slants up toward the center back seam. The opening is finished with a narrow topstitched hem.

Pattern Development:

1. Enlarge the pocket pattern above.

2. Add a 1" hem allowance and 1/2" seam allowances. Indicate the grainline.

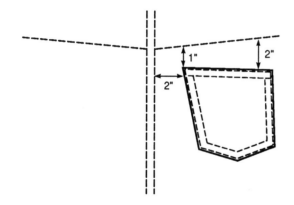

1"

2"

2"

Sewing Notes:

1. Use orange or gold topstitching thread on the bobbin and navy regular thread in the needle. Adjust the tension. Stitching underside up, finish the opening with a machine-stitched double-fold hem and edgestitch the opening.

2. Press the seam allowances to the wrong side and trim them to a skinny 1/2".

3. Baste the pocket in place so the right hip pocket is positioned as shown.

4. Rethread the needle with orange top-stitching thread and the bobbin with navy regular thread. Adjust the tension. Set the pocket with a row of edgestitching and a row of topstitching 1/2" from the edge. The seam allowances should be enclosed between the two rows of stitching.

Unlined Pocket With Tucked Hem

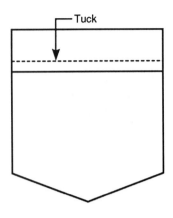

Tuck

Design Analysis:

At first glance this pocket looks like it is finished with a straight wrong-side-out hem, but, unlike the wrong-side-out variation, it doesn't require fabrics which are attractive on the reverse side. Well-suited for garments made of lightweight fabrics which will be laundered frequently, the tucked hem is particularly attractive when the same finish is used on short sleeves.

In these directions, the hem depth is 1-1/4" deep with a 1/4" tuck. The tuck encases the raw edge of the hem allowance. You can vary the depths of the hem and/or the tuck.

For more information on tucks, see Tuck Terminology on page 50.

Pattern Development:

1. Use a commercial pattern or the Basic Unlined Pocket pattern (see page 2). Draw the tuck foldline 1-1/4" below the opening. Draw a matchpoint on the foldline 1" from the left side. Draw the tuck stitching line 1/4" above the foldline.

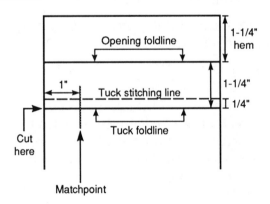

Measure the hem allowance. If it isn't 1-1/4", add or subtract as needed.

2. Make the tuck strip on another piece of pattern paper wider than the pocket. Draw two parallel lines twice the tuck width (here, 1/2") plus a small amount to allow for the turn of the cloth.

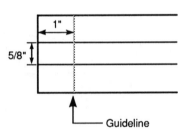

 Hint: *For very lightweight fabrics, a fat 1/8" works well; for slightly heavier fabrics, add 1/4". For these directions, draw the tuck strip 5/8".*

Draw a guideline perpendicular to the first two lines 1" from the left side.

3. Cut the pocket pattern on the tuck foldline.

4. Tape the tuck strip between the pocket pieces, aligning the matchpoints with the guideline and the cut edges with the horizontal lines.

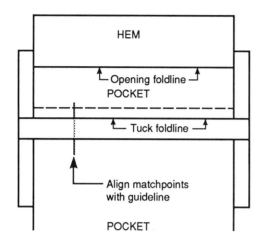

HEM

─ Opening foldline ─┐
POCKET

─ Tuck foldline ─┘

─ Align matchpoints with guideline

POCKET

5. Fold the paper pocket so that the hem and tuck are in their finished positions. Cut out the pattern, trimming off the excess paper at the sides and bottom.

Sewing Notes:

1. Cut one pocket. Mark the ends of the pocket foldline with clips.

2. Wrong sides together, fold first at the pocket foldline and fold again to the wrong side. This encases the raw edge of the hem allowance.

3. With the folded hem of the pocket up, stitch the tuck 1/4" from the folded edge.

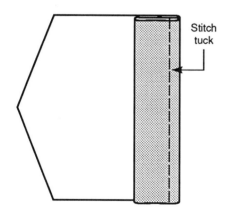

Stitch tuck

4. Press hem and tuck flat. Complete the pocket and apply it to the garment.

Unlined Pocket With Band

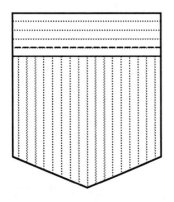

Design Analysis:

Frequently used to create novelty designs on patterned fabrics, the banded opening is also an attractive finish for pockets with inverted pleats, box pleats, tucks, gathers, and slot seams. These directions are for a straight 1"-deep band; however, the band can be deeper, narrower, or shaped to repeat other elements of the design.

See also page 70, Pleated Pocket with Shaped Band.

Pattern Development:

1. Draw the band/pocket seamline on your Basic Unlined Pocket pattern (see page 2). Indicate a matchpoint on the seamline.

Indicate the grainline on both the pocket and the band. Both grainlines can be perpendicular to the opening; however, the grainline on the band is usually parallel to the opening on plain or striped fabrics. On plaid fabrics, a bias band is attractive.

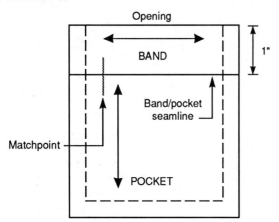

2. *Pocket pattern:* On another piece of paper, trace the pocket section, the cutting lines at the sides and bottom, and the grainline. Add a 5/8" seam allowance to the pocket/band seamline. Transfer the matchpoint to the cutting line.

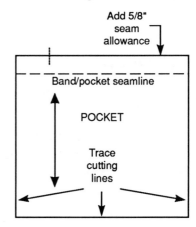

3. *Band pattern:* Use a piece of pattern paper more than twice the depth of the band and wider than the pocket. Fold the paper in half lengthwise. Align the fold on the paper with the pocket opening. Trace the band. Add seam allowances to the band/pocket seamline.

Transfer the matchpoint to the seam allowance raw edge. Indicate the grainline. Cut out the pattern on the cutting lines.

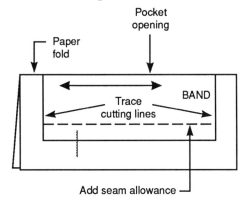

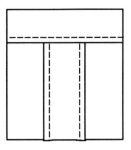

Tucks

Sewing Notes for Unlined Pocket:

1. Cut one pocket and one band. Mark the ends of the band foldline with clips.

2. Right side of band to wrong side of pocket, join the pocket and band. Trim the seam to 1/4"; press toward the band.

3. Wrong sides together, fold and press the band at the foldline. Press the long raw edge of the band under a skinny 5/8". Baste. From the right side, edgestitch the band in place.

4. Complete and set the pocket.

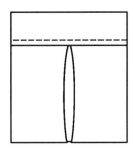

Inverted pleat

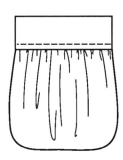

Gathers

Modification for Lined Pocket:

1. Cut one pocket, one pocket lining, and one band. Mark the ends of the band foldline with clips.

2. Right sides together, join the sides and bottom of the pocket and lining; trim. Turn right side out and press.

3. Right side of band to wrong side of pocket, stitch the seam. Trim the seam to 1/4"; press towards the band. Finish the ends of the band, right sides together. Trim, turn right side out, and press.

4. Fold the raw edge under a skinny 5/8" and edgestitch.

5. Complete and set the pocket.

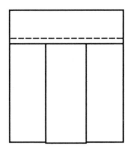

Box pleat

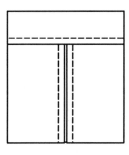

Slot seams

Gathered Pocket With Band

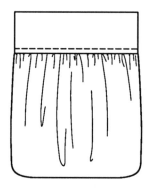

Design Analysis:

Particularly attractive in soft fabrics, this pocket can be lined or unlined. The gathered pouch is smoothly finished with a straight band.

Pattern Development:

1. Decide how deep you want the band. Then draw the band/pocket seamline on a tracing of your Basic Unlined Pocket pattern (see page 2). Indicate matchpoints about 1/2" from each end and cut the pattern apart on the band/pocket seamline. Indicate the grainline on both parts.

2. *Band pattern:* Tape the band section to another piece of paper and finish the band pattern, using the directions on page 10.

3. *Pocket pattern:* Trim away any seam allowances and cut the pattern in half vertically. Discard one half. Beginning at the top, make several vertical slashes to-but-not-through the bottom seamline.

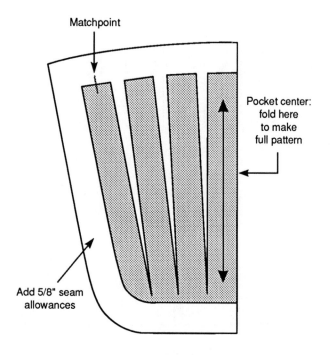

Matchpoint

Pocket center: fold here to make full pattern

Add 5/8" seam allowances

4. On another piece of paper, draw a vertical line for the pocket center and grainline. Align the center of the slashed pattern on the drawn line. Tape the pocket centers together. Spread the slashed pocket 1/4" to 3/4" at each of the slashes. Tape in place. Draw a smooth line across the top and bottom of the pattern and add seam allowances to all edges.

5. Fold the tracing paper over the pocket at the center and trace the cutting lines. *Optional:* To make a clean pattern, trace the cutting lines, matchpoints, and grainline.

Sewing Notes:

1. Cut one pocket and one band. Mark the band foldline and the pocket and band centers with clips.

2. Loosen upper tension. Then, wrong side up, place a row of ease basting just inside the seamline at the top of the pocket. Place another row midway between the seamline and raw edge.

3. Right side of band against wrong side of pocket, match and pin the raw edges and matchpoints. Pull up and adjust the gathers; stitch. Trim the band seam allowance a fat 1/4". Trim the pocket seam allowance a skinny 1/4". Press toward band.

4. Fold and press the band at the foldline. Press under the raw edge a skinny 5/8". Baste. Edgestitch the band in place.

5. Complete and set the pocket.

Faced Edges

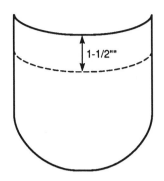

Design Analysis:

The separate facing can be used on edges which are shaped, as well as when the facing is used as a decorative trim.

These directions are for a facing finished 1-1/2"-wide.

Pattern Development:

1. Outline the pocket and draw the facing on the pattern.

2. *Pocket pattern:* Add seam allowances to all edges and indicate the grainline.

3. *Facing pattern:* Trace the cutting lines of the pocket pattern and the new facing line. Indicate the grainline and add a 1/4" seam allowance to the bottom of the facing.

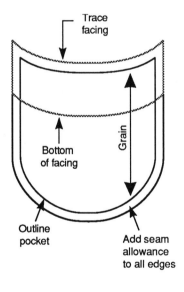

Sewing Notes:

1. Cut one pocket and one facing.

2. Finish the lower edge of the facing (see pages 100).

3. Right sides together, join the facing and pocket at the top.

4. Press the seam toward the facing. Understitch and trim the seam to 1/4".

5. Right sides together, stitch the sides of the facing and pocket. Trim, press, and turn the facing to the inside. Baste.

6. Complete and set the pocket to the garment.

Unlined Pocket With Ribbon Facing

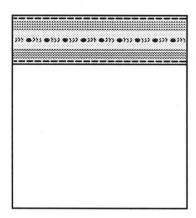

Design Analysis:

Frequently used on cardigan jackets trimmed with ribbon, single-ply braid, or even lace, this pocket is easy to make. On most designs, a 1"-wide trim will be attractive; however, the trim width can vary from 5/8" to 2".

Pattern Development:

1. When using a commercial pattern or the Basic Unlined Pocket pattern, trim the hem allowance to 5/8".

2. To determine the yardage requirements for the ribbon, measure the width of the pocket opening including the seam allowances.

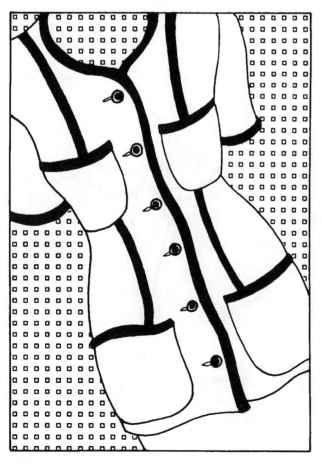

Sewing Notes:

1. Cut one pocket from the fashion fabric.

2. At the top of the pocket, mark with chalk or machine stitching just inside the seamline.

3. Right side of ribbon against wrong side of pocket, position the ribbon edge so it barely covers the marked seamline. Baste. Edgestitch the ribbon in place. Trim the seam allowance to 1/4".

4. Fold and press the ribbon to the right side of the pocket. Baste. Edgestitch the lower edge of the ribbon to the pocket.

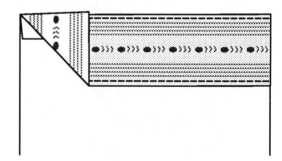

5. Set the pocket to the garment.

Decorative Faced Opening

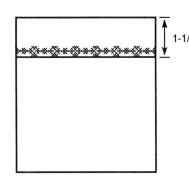

1-1/2"

Design Analysis:

The Faced Opening frequently looks like a wrong-side-out hem; however, it isn't dependent on the fabric having an attractive wrong side. The decorative facing can be cut on a different grain or from a different fabric; it can be straight or shaped.

These directions are for a 1-1/2"-wide straight facing.

Pattern Development:

1. Using a commercial pattern or the Basic Unlined Pocket pattern, draw the facing on the pattern. Draw a seam allowance at the pocket opening and trim away any remaining hem allowance.

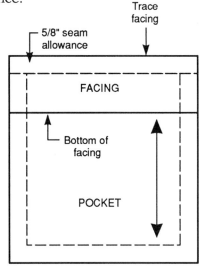

5/8" seam allowance

Trace facing

FACING

Bottom of facing

POCKET

2. *Pocket pattern:* On a piece of pattern paper, trace the pocket cutting lines and grainline.

3. *Facing pattern:* Trace the facing cutting lines at the top and sides. Indicate the grainline and add a seam allowance to the bottom of the facing.

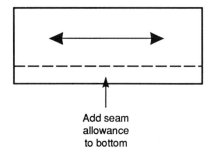

Add seam allowance to bottom

Hint: *Be adventurous. When working with stripes, the usual choice is to draw the grainline parallel to the opening. Instead, design the facing with a point, add a seam at the center, and draw the grainline parallel to the lower edges.*

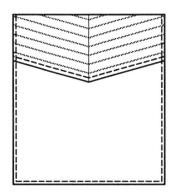

Sewing Notes:

1. Cut one pocket and one facing.

2. On the facing, staystitch the lower edge just inside the seamline; press the seam allowance under so the stitched line barely shows on the wrong side.

Hint: *For a novelty finish, face the facing. Cut a second facing from self-fabric or a lightweight material. Then, right sides together, join the lower edges. Trim and turn the facing right side out and press.*

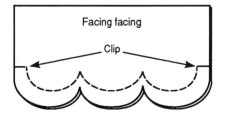

Facing facing

Clip

3. At the opening, right side of facing to wrong side of pocket, join the facing and pocket.

4. Press the seam toward the pocket. Understitch pocket and trim the seam to 1/4".

5. Right sides up, fold the facing in place. Baste and edgestitch.

 ***Hint:*** *On some designs, I appliqué the facing in place. First straight stitch (L,1) on the design line; trim close to the stitched line. Then, using a medium-width satin stitch (W,2-L.25), stitch the facing in place.*

6. Complete and set the pocket to the garment.

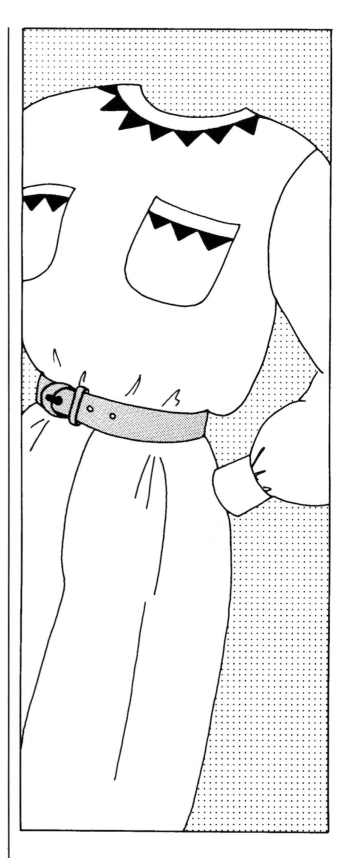

Elasticized Opening

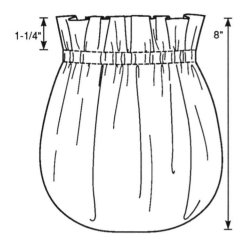

Design Analysis:

This novelty pocket has a self-faced ruffle above the elastic casing. It's a nice roomy pocket, even when it's made in a smaller size, and little girls particularly like it.

The finished pocket in these directions is 8" by 8". It has 1-1/4" ruffle with a 1/2"-wide casing. It requires a 1/4" - 3/8" wide braided elastic.

Other variations of the pocket can be developed by locating the elastic at the top of the pocket to create a novelty design or a utilitarian pocket for tennis balls (see page 18).

Pattern Development:

This pattern is easier to develop when you start with a half pattern.

1. *Pocket pattern:* Draw a 4" by 8" rectangle. Label the right side "pocket center" and round the lower left corner.

2. Draw three lines parallel to the center. Cut out the pocket.

3. Cut each line beginning at the pocket opening and ending about 1/16" from the bottom.

4. Fold another piece of pattern paper in half vertically. Align and tape the pocket center to the foldline. Spread the pattern 1/2" to 3/4" at each slash and tape the pattern in place.

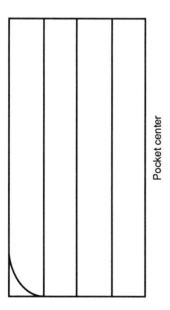

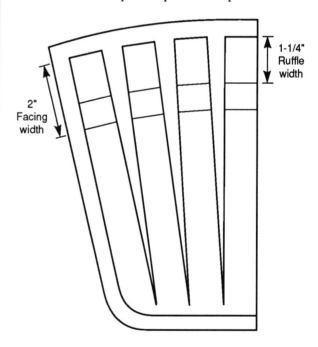

5. Redraw the curve at the bottom and sides so it will be a smooth line.

6. Draw the width of the ruffle (1-1/4") below the top of the pocket.

7. Using a red pencil or short dashes, outline the facing on the pocket 2" below the top.

8. Add seam allowances to all edges and draw the grainline parallel to the center of the pocket.

9. *Facing pattern:* Trace all cutting lines, and the grainline.

Sewing Notes:

1. Cut one pocket and one facing.

2. Right sides together, join the pocket and the facing. Press, understitch, and trim.

3. Wrong side up, press the seam allowances to the wrong side. Fold facing to underside and press.

4. Fold the raw edge of the facing under 1/4" and edgestitch it in place. Stitch again 1/2" away to make the casing.

5. Select a braided elastic 1/4" – 3/8" wide. Measure and mark two lengths, each 7" and 9" from one end. Using a bodkin or small safety pin, insert the elastic into the casing. Pin one end at the seam allowance. Pull the elastic and align the first mark with the other raw edge. Examine the pocket: do you like the look? Then align the edge with the other mark. Examine the pocket again.

When the elastic is longer, the pocket will be very rectangular; when the elastic is shortened, the pocket will be smaller at the top. You are the designer, so you can select the look you like.

 Hint: Once you've determined the elastic length, baste just inside the seamline so the ends won't get lost.

When making a pair of pockets, be sure the elastic is the same length in both so the pockets will be identical.

6. Right sides up, pin the pocket in place. Let the pocket pull in at the sides. Edgestitch.

 Hint: Check to be sure the garment is flat under the pocket with stretch only at the top of the pocket.

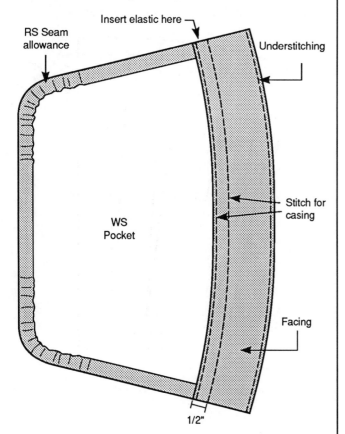

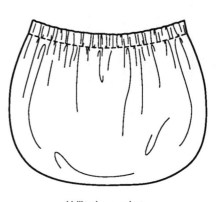

Utilitarian pocket

Gathered Pouch

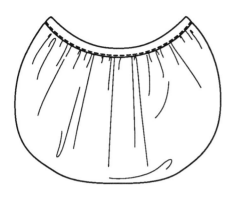

Design Analysis:

A favorite of little girls, this pocket is a variation of the elasticized pocket. However, since the edges are longer than the center, the pocket dips at the center.

These directions are for a smaller 5" by 5" pocket finished with a 1/4"-wide bias binding at the opening.

Pattern Development:

This pattern is also easier to develop when you start with a half pattern.

1. *Pocket pattern:* Draw a 2-1/2" by 5" rectangle. Label the right side "pocket center." Round the lower left corner.

2. Slash and spread the pattern 1/2" to 3/4" at each slash, as indicated in Steps 3 and 4 on page 17, until the pattern measures 5".

3. To draw the pocket opening, square a line from the center to the upper left corner. Redraw the curve at the bottom and sides so it will be a smooth line.

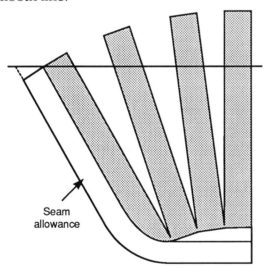

Seam allowance

4. Add seam allowances to the sides and bottom.

5. *Binding pattern:* Draw a rectangle 1-1/4" deep and 6-1/4" wide. (These measurements are five times the finished width and the finished length plus two seam allowances.) This will be a bias strip, so indicate the grainline.

Sewing Notes:

1. Cut one pocket and one length of binding.

2. Wrong side up, press the seam allowances at the sides and bottom of the pocket to the wrong side.

3. Mark the center of the pocket opening.

4. Place two gathering rows 1/4" and 3/16" from the raw edge of the opening.

 Hint: *For easier gathering, use a regular stitch length and loosen the tension on the needle thread.*

5. Mark the center of the bias strip and 5/8" from each end. Turn in the ends of the bias strip at your two end marks and press.

6. Right sides together, pin the binding to the pocket, aligning the center marks. Pull up the gathers on the pocket so it matches the finished length of the bias strip.

Stitch 1/4" (the width of the finished binding) from the edge.

Press the binding toward the opening; wrap it over the raw edge and press again.

Right side up, ditch stitch or topstitch the binding permanently.

7. Edgestitch the pocket in place.

2. Lined Patch Pockets

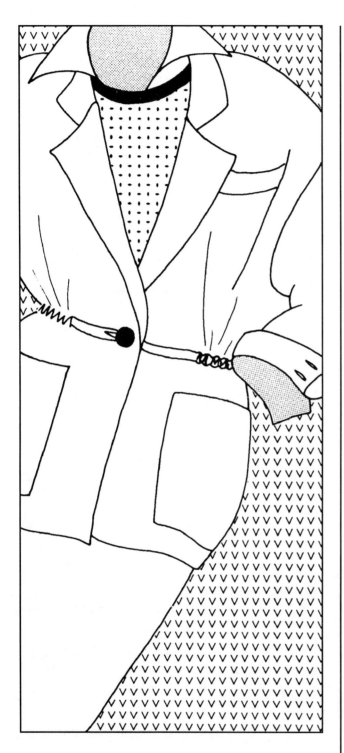

Generally, lined pockets are more attractive and wear better than unlined pockets. They are particularly well-suited for transparent, soft, loosely woven, and medium- to heavy-weight fabrics, as well as bias-cut designs, novelty pockets with unusual shapes, and tailored garments.

The best lining choices are lightweight self-fabrics or traditional lining materials; however, a variety of coordinating fabrics can be used for design. When sewing printed transparent fabrics, solid color linings are usually best. Although linings add opaqueness to transparent fabrics, they should not be used as a substitute for interfacing.

When creating original designs, consider the pocket use, design, application, fashion fabric, and garment quality before choosing the lining method. If the pocket will be applied with topstitching 1/4" or more from the edge, use an edge-to-edge lining made of self-fabric or an attractive companion fabric for the lining material (page 27); bind the pocket edges so they'll also be attractive on the underside (page 32) ; cut the pocket seam allowances wider; or apply the lining by hand so it won't show (page 24). If the pocket will be inside-stitched (page 39), flat-line it (page 26); if it will be fake inside-stitched (page 34), use an edge-to-edge lining (page 28). If it will receive hard wear, use the Magic-Lined Pocket (page 35).

Linings are usually cut on the same grain as the pocket. Be sure to preshrink your lining materials.

Be sure to read the General Directions on page 91 for information on interfacings, finishes, and setting of pockets.

Basic Lined Pocket

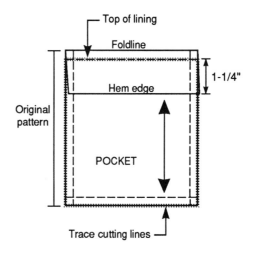

Underside

Pocket hem

1"

Lining

Grain of lining parallel to opening

Design Analysis:

The Basic Lined Pocket is the most popular patch design on tailored garments. Pocket sizes vary with the length and size of the garment, as well as the size of the wearer.

On most single-breasted jackets and coats, the pockets are located about 3" – 3-1/2" from the front edge and parallel to it. On double-breasted designs, the pocket is usually parallel to the garment dart.

The finished pocket can have square or rounded corners. It is usually longer than it is wide. On this pocket, seam allowances are 5/8" and the hem allowance is 1-1/2".

The pocket lining is a lightweight fabric and slightly smaller than the pocket itself. On the finished pocket, the lining begins about 7/8" below the pocket opening. If you have not interfaced the pocket opening, the pocket will hold its shape better if the lining is cut with the grain parallel to the opening.

The tops of the pocket and lining are first joined by machine, with an opening left at the center for turning. After the remaining edges are machine-stitched, the pocket is turned right-side-out and sewn to the garment.

Pattern Development for Pocket Lining:

If the design doesn't have a lining pattern or if you're creating a new pocket design, use these directions to make a pocket lining pattern.

1. Fold the pocket pattern at the foldline.

2. To establish the cutting line of the lining pattern, begin at the hem edge, not the foldline. Measure and mark a line 1-1/4" above it, using a red pencil or broken line. This equals two seam allowances.

3. Make the lining pattern on another piece of paper. Trace the cutting lines of the pocket to the top of the lining pattern (broken line). Trace the pocket grainline.

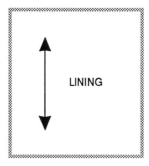

Top of lining

Foldline

Hem edge

1-1/4"

Original pattern

POCKET

Trace cutting lines

LINING

Sewing Notes:

1. Cut one pocket and one pocket lining. On the pocket, mark the ends of the pocket foldline with short clips. Interface the pocket as needed (see page 94).

2. Right sides together, join the pocket and lining at the top with a 5/8" seam, leaving a 2" opening at the center.

3. Press the seam flat, then toward the lining.

4. Grade the seam as needed. For a more attractive pocket, trim all the edges of the lining 1/8", tapering to nothing at the pocket foldline.

5. Right sides together, fold the pocket at the foldline. Join the sides and bottom, stretching the hemline.

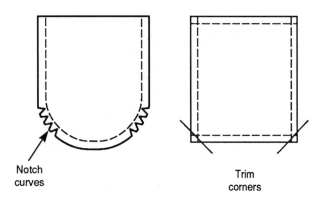 *Hints: Beginning at the bottom, match and pin the raw edges together so the pocket bubbles at the center. Starting at the foldline, stitch a 5/8" seam, tapering out to 1/2" at the bottom of the hem allowance. The pocket seam allowance is 5/8". But, once you've trimmed the lining, some fabric will be lost when the pocket is turned right-side-out. On most fabrics, you'll lose about 1/8".*

On heavy or bulky fabrics, the loss is even greater. To compensate, stitch only a 3/8" seam.

Shorten the stitch length for greater accuracy and for a more durable pocket.

Notch
curves

Trim
corners

6. Trim the seam to a skinny 1/4". To remove excess bulk, notch the curves or trim corners.

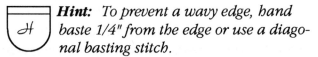 *Hints: On better garments, press the seams open before trimming. Then trim the lining seam allowances to 1/8" and the pocket seam allowances to 1/4".*

To press, begin lining side up. Open the seam and press the lining seam allowance toward the lining itself. Turn the pocket over and repeat for the pocket. See page 106.

7. Turn the pocket right-side-out through the opening at the top of the lining. On better garments, close the opening with a slipstitch; on everyday garments, close the opening with a strip of fusible web, permanent glue, or just leave it open.

8. Lining side up, baste around the pocket so the seamline is barely visible at the edge. Press, wrong side up.

Hint: To prevent a wavy edge, hand baste 1/4" from the edge or use a diagonal basting stitch.

9. Topstitch the pocket opening if desired and complete any decorative stitching.

10. Right side up, baste the pocket in place. For your finest designs, hand baste with a small diagonal stitch or double basting. On everyday garments, speed baste with pins, washable glue, water-soluble double-stick tape, or fusible web.

11. Set the pocket to the garment by edgestitching 1/16" from the pocket edge, topstitching at the edge and again 1/4", or hand sewing it. (See page 102).

Easy Lined Pocket

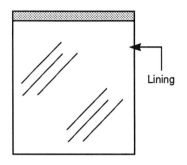

Lining

Design Analysis:

This Easy Lined Pocket is a variation of the Basic Lined Pocket. Unlike the Basic Lined Pocket, both the pocket and lining are cut by the pocket pattern and the tops of the two sections are not joined by machine.

Pattern Development:

Use the information for the Basic Lined Pocket on page 21.

Sewing Notes:

1. Use the pocket pattern to cut one pocket from the fashion fabric and one from the lining material. On each section, mark the ends of the foldline with short clips. Interface the pocket as needed.

 Hint: *Cut the top of the pocket lining on the selvage so it will stay the opening.*

2. Wrong sides together, fold and pin the pocket hem at the clips. Wrong sides together, fold and pin the pocket hem allowance plus 1/4"; press. Trim the sides and bottom 1/8".

3. Right sides together, match and pin the edges of the pocket and lining together so the lining fold is 1/4" below the marked opening. Stitch three sides, press, and trim.

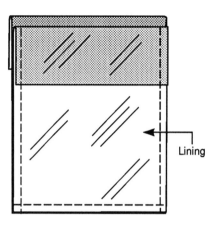

Lining

 Hint: *Stitch with the lining on top so the feed dogs will ease the fashion fabric into the seamline.*

4. Turn the pocket right side out.

5. Lining side up, baste around the pocket so the seamline is barely visible at the edge. Press.

6. Close the opening at the top of the pocket by hand or with a small bit of fusible web.

7. Set the pocket.

Couture Lined Pocket

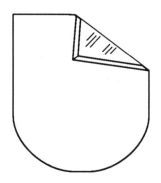

Design Analysis:

The couture method is only used on the finest garments. The pocket is assembled before the lining is cut. Then the lining is sewn to the pocket by hand.

Pattern Development:

Use the information for the Basic Lined Pocket on page 21.

Sewing Notes:

1. Cut one pocket from the fashion fabric. Mark all finished edges (hem and seamlines) with thread tracing. Do not cut the lining.

2. Interface the pocket as needed.

3. Topstitch if desired. You have more control if you topstitch before applying the pocket to the garment.

 Hint: Mark the topstitching lines with chalk or thread tracing.

4. Place a line of hand ease basting at each curve midway between the seamline and raw edge.

5. Pull up the ease basting so the thread tracing barely shows on the wrong side of the pocket. Baste around the pocket 1/4" from the edges.

Hint: On the sides of the pocket hem, fold seam allowances under about 3/4" so the lining will cover all raw edges and stray threads.

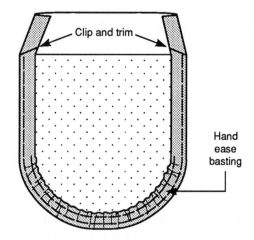

Clip and trim

Hand ease basting

6. Wrong side up, press. Trim and notch the seam allowances.

Hint: Trim away excess bulk at the corners and, if necessary, spank the edges briskly with the clapper so they will be flat and smooth.

7. Wrong sides together, fold and baste the pocket hem in place.

8. Wrong sides together, place the pocket on a rectangle of lining fabric, matching the grainlines. Pin the centers together. Trim the lining so that it extends 1/8" at each edge.

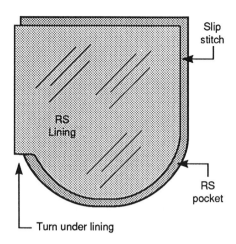

Slip stitch

RS Lining

RS pocket

Turn under lining

9. Lining side up, fold the raw edges of the lining under so you can see about 1/8" of the pocket fabric at each edge. Baste. Then fell or slipstitch the lining in place. Press lightly and remove the bastings.

10. Right side up, cover the pocket with a press cloth. Press lightly with a steam iron.

11. Right sides up, pin the pocket to the garment. Then baste about 1/4" from the edge. Turn the garment wrong side up and secure the pocket with short running stitches or small diagonal stitches.

Hint: *If the pocket is more for looks than use, use the faster running stitch. To make it slightly more secure, use a running stitch again to fill in the spaces of the first row. For heavier duty, use diagonal stitches, but remember, this is a couture technique and you won't be carrying rocks in your pocket, I hope.*

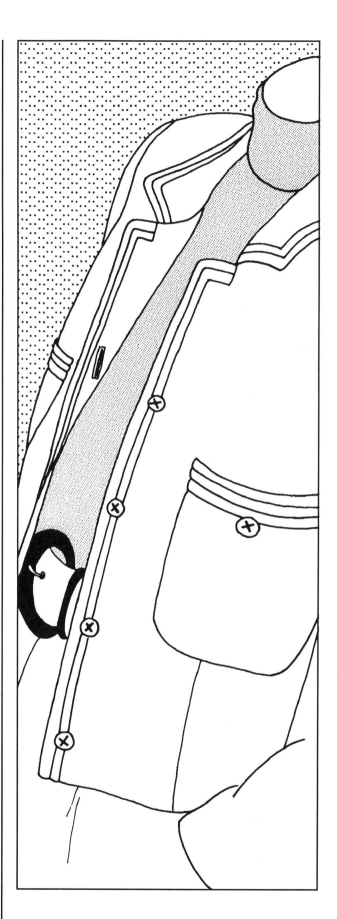

Flat-Lined Pocket

Underside

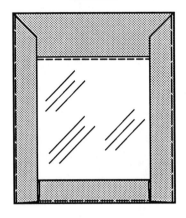

Design Analysis:

Frequently used for Inside-Stitched (page 39) and Bellows Pockets (page 71), Flat-Lined Pockets are more durable and luxurious than their unlined cousins.

The lining is stitched to the pocket hem right sides together so that it finishes the raw edge of the hem. The remaining edges—sides and bottom—are left raw or finished with serging.

Pattern Development:

If a lining pattern isn't provided, use the one for the Basic Lined Pocket with a 1-1/2" hem. Later, you will trim away the excess. (See page 21.)

Sewing Notes:

1. Cut the pocket and mark the foldline with clips on each side.

2. Cut the pocket lining.

3. Interface the pocket as needed.

4. Right sides together, join the lining and pocket at the hem. Press the seam toward the lining and understitch.

5. Wrong sides together, fold the pocket at the foldline, using the clips as a guide.

6. Machine baste the raw edges together just inside the seamline or serge the edges together.

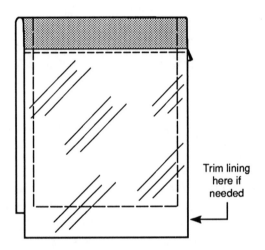

Trim lining here if needed

Hint: If you have cut the lining by the pocket pattern, it will extend below the pocket. Just trim it away after you baste or when you serge.

7. If the pocket will be inside-stitched (see page 39), set the pocket to the garment. If it will be set by another application, press the seam allowances to the wrong side; then set the pocket.

Hints: Be precise when pressing—use a template or Pocket Former.

Fold in the corners of the seam allowance at the opening so the raw edges won't show on the garment. See the Shirt Method on page 3.

Decorative Edge-to-Edge Lining

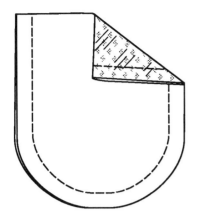

Design Analysis:

The Decorative Edge-to-Edge Lining is used for pockets with unusual shapes, curves, and scallops; designs which utilize the lining fabric as part of the design; and Fake Inside-Stitched Pockets (page 34).

The decorative lining is cut exactly the same size as the pocket, from self-fabric or an attractive companion fabric. All edges are machine-stitched, and the lining is slashed so the pocket can be turned. On the finished pocket, the lining extends to all edges so the lining or pocket application can be used as a decorative detail on the garment.

Pattern Development:

1. *Pocket pattern:* Outline the finished pocket, indicate the grainline, and add seam allowances to all edges. You will not need a hem on this pocket.

 Hint: *Generally, I add 1/4" seam allowances, which are easy to stitch accurately.*

2. *Lining pattern:* Use the pocket pattern.

Sewing Notes:

1. Cut the pocket from the fashion fabric. Cut the pocket lining from self-fabric or an attractive companion fabric.

2. Right sides together, pin edges of the pocket and lining together. Stitch around the pocket and trim as needed. Press.

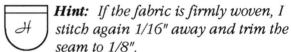 **Hint:** *If the fabric is firmly woven, I stitch again 1/16" away and trim the seam to 1/8".*

3. Make a short bias slash on the lining at the bottom of the pocket.

4. Turn the pocket right-side-out.

5. Close the slash by hand, by slipping a small piece of fusible web under it, or just leave it open.

6. Press the pocket so the seamline is right at the edge. You will be able to see the lining somewhat.

7. Set the pocket with topstitching 1/4" to 1" from the edges.

Utilitarian Edge-to-Edge Lining

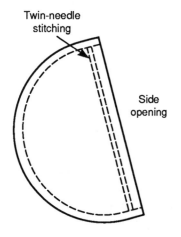

Twin-needle stitching

Side opening

Design Analysis:

Like the Decorative Edge-to-Edge Lining, the Utilitarian Edge-to-Edge lining is also used for pockets with unusual shapes, curves, and scallops.

Cut from lightweight lining fabric, the utilitarian lining is slightly smaller than the pocket itself so the seamlines at the edges won't show on the finished garment. All edges are machine-stitched and the lining is slashed so the pocket can be turned.

Pattern Development:

1. *Pocket pattern:* Outline the finished pocket. Indicate the grainline and add seam allowances to all edges.

 Hint: *Generally, I add 1/4" seam allowances, which are easy to stitch accurately.*

2. *Lining pattern:* Trace the pocket pattern and trim all edges 1/8".

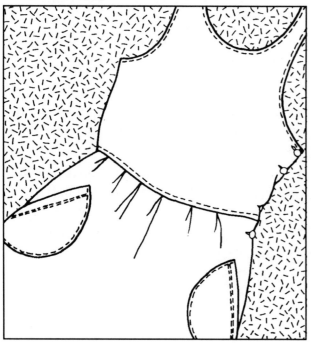

Sewing Notes:

1. Cut the pocket from the fashion fabric. Cut the pocket lining from lining fabric.

2. Right sides together, pin the top edges of the pocket and lining together. Stitch. Then understitch and trim as needed. Press.

3. Right sides together, match and pin the remaining edges together. Stitch and trim as needed.

 Hint: *If the fabric is firmly woven, I stitch again 1/16" away and trim the seam to 1/8".*

4. Make a short bias slash on the lining at the bottom of the pocket.

5. Turn the pocket right-side-out.

6. Close the slash by hand or just leave it open.

7. Wrong side up, press the pocket so the seamline is barely visible at the edge.

8. Set the pocket with edgestitching.

Variation: Utilitarian Edge-to-Edge Lining—Hook Method

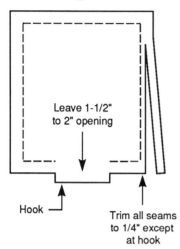

Leave 1-1/2" to 2" opening

Hook

Trim all seams to 1/4" except at hook

Design Analysis:

On this variation for a Utilitarian Edge-to-Edge Lining, the hook—an extended seam allowance—is left at the bottom of the pocket.

Pattern Development:

Use the instructions for Utilitarian Edge-to-Edge Lining on page 28.

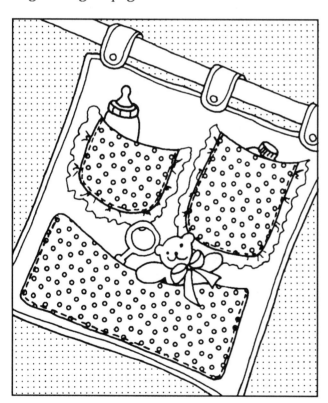

Sewing Notes:

1. Cut the pocket from the fashion fabric. Cut the pocket lining from a lightweight lining material.

 Hint: *When using the hook method, I prefer 5/8" seam allowances.*

2. Right sides together, pin the tops of the pocket and lining together. Stitch. Understitch and trim. Press.

3. Right sides together, match and pin the remaining edges around the pocket. Stitch, leaving a 1-1/2" – 2" opening on the bottom edge.

4. Trim the seams to 1/4", except at the hook—the unstitched area. Grade the seams as needed.

5. Turn the pocket right-side-out and press.

6. Wrong side up, press the pocket, rolling the seamline to the under side.

7. Set the pocket. When the pocket is edge-stitched or topstitched 1/4" from the edge, the opening at the bottom will be secured.

One-Piece Self-Lined Pocket

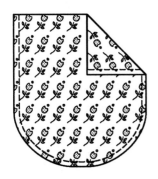

Design Analysis:

Suitable for light- to medium-weight fabrics, this pocket is particularly attractive on casual designs and children's wear.

The pocket and lining are cut all-in-one-piece and have a foldline at the opening. They can be interfaced but frequently are not. The lining half can be trimmed so the seamlines will roll to the underside; however, the pocket can also be assembled without trimming the lining to achieve special effects.

Pattern Development:

1. Fold the tracing paper in half horizontally. With the pocket opening located at the fold, outline the finished pocket.

2. Add seam allowances and indicate the grainline. Cut out the pattern.

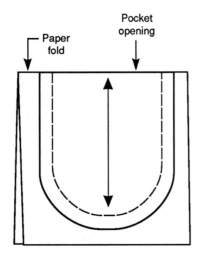

Hints: *If I plan to turn the pocket through a slash, I add 1/4" seam allowances, which are easier to stitch accurately than 5/8" seams. This also eliminates the need to trim later.*

If I plan to turn through a hook (see page 29), I prefer wider seam allowances.

Sewing Notes:

1. Cut one pocket/lining. Mark the foldline with short clips.

2. Right sides together, fold the pocket at the foldline. Match and pin the raw edges. Stitch around the pocket on the seamline, beginning and ending with a backstitch.

Hints: *Before stitching, trim the edges of the lining section 1/8", tapering to nothing at the foldline, if you want the seamline to roll to the underside.*

For special effects when setting the pocket, do not trim the lining so the seamline will be at the pocket edges.

3. Trim the seam allowances as needed.

Hint: *If the fabric is firmly woven, stitch again 1/16" away and trim the seam to 1/8".*

4. Make a short slash in the pocket lining near the bottom of the pocket. If the fabric doesn't ravel, make a vertical slash; if it does, make the slash on the bias.

5. Turn the pocket right-side-out through the slash.

6. Close the slash with a loose diagonal stitch or a small rectangle of fusible interfacing. Or, if the pocket is decorative or will receive little or no use, leave the slash open and forget it.

7. Wrong side up, press, rolling the seamlines at the edges toward the lining if desired.

8. Set the pocket. For an inconspicuous finish, edgestitch around the pocket. For special effects, topstitch 1/4" to 1" from the edge; use multiple rows of stitching to correspond with other details on the design; stitch a design that doesn't parallel the edges of the pocket; or stitch the pocket "invisibly" (See page 34).

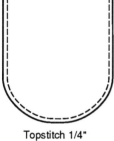 *Hint: Mark the stitching lines with a chalk or tape a paper template to the pocket. Then machine stitch the pocket to the garment.*

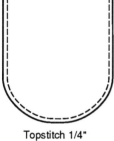

Topstitch 1/4"
from edge

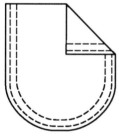

Use multiple rows

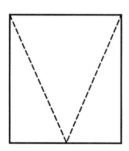

Topstitch a
different design

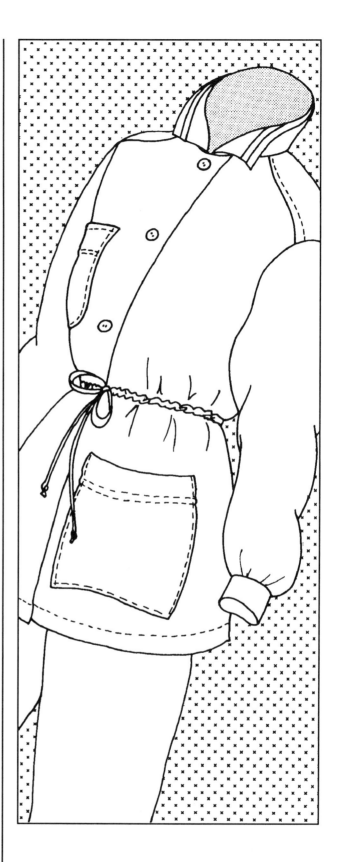

Self-Lined Pocket With Bound Edge

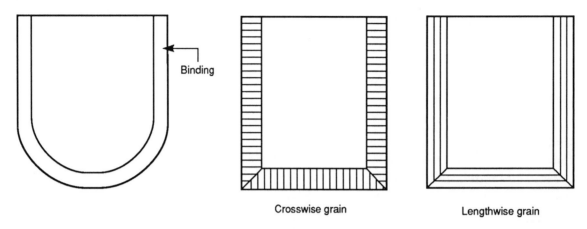

Binding

Crosswise grain

Lengthwise grain

Design Analysis:

This Self-Lined Pocket has a fold at the opening edge. Then the sides and bottom are finished with a binding. Since the binding will be easier to shape on curved edges, it is usually cut on the bias, but it can be on the lengthwise grain or crossgrain. On this pocket, the binding is finished 1/2" wide; however, it could be wider or narrower or be replaced by foldover braid or ribbon. It can also be bound on four sides, instead of three.

Pattern Development:

1. *Pocket and lining pattern:* Fold the pattern paper in half. Outline the finished pocket with the opening on the folded line. Draw the binding trim on the remaining three edges.

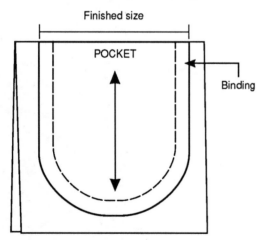

Finished size

POCKET

Binding

2. Cut out the pocket pattern on the finished size and indicate the grainline. Since the edges will be bound, the pocket doesn't need seam allowances.

3. *Binding strip:* Draw a strip four times the finished width. For a 1/2"-wide binding, draw the strip 2" wide. Indicate the grainline. If the pocket is shaped, bias bindings are easier to shape. (See Establishing the Bias on page *x*.)

To determine the length of the strip, measure all edges to be bound and add 5".

Hint: If you plan to use purchased binding, ribbon, or braid, you won't need a pattern for the binding. Measure the pocket to determine the amount needed and indicate it on the pocket pattern.

Sewing Notes:

1. Cut one pocket/lining. Mark the foldline with short clips. From self-fabric or a complementary fabric, cut the binding the desired length and grain.

2. Wrong sides together, fold the pocket at the notches. Baste the edges together 1/4" from edge.

3. To apply the binding, begin at the upper right corner. Right sides together, match the raw edges, letting the binding extend 1" above the pocket.

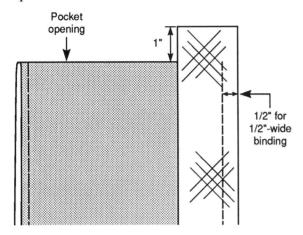

4. Use the width of the finished binding as the seam allowance. For a 1/2"-wide binding, stitch 1/2" from the raw edges.

Hints: If the pocket is curved at the bottom, you must ease the binding around the curves because the length of the stitching line is shorter than the length of the pocket edge. If you are unsure, baste the binding at the curves and check to be sure it fits the pocket edge smoothly.

If the pocket has squared corners, stitch toward the corner, stopping 1/2" or the finished binding width from the bottom of the pocket. Backstitch and break your threads.

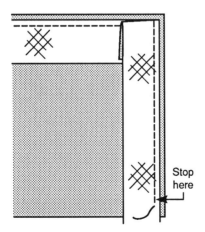

Refold the bias, aligning the bias with the bottom of the pocket and stitch. Repeat for the other corner.

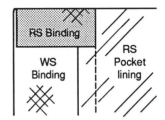

5. Press the binding toward the pocket edges. At the pocket opening, fold the binding ends to the wrong side. Pin them in place.

6. Wrap the binding around the pocket edges and pin close to the binding/pocket seam. Press; then ditch stitch to hold the binding in place. Trim the binding on the underside close to the basting.

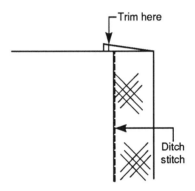

7. Right sides up, pin the pocket in place. Place the pins in the center of the pocket so you can stitch without removing them.

8. To set the pocket, ditch stitch with regular thread where the binding joins the pocket.

Fake Inside-Stitched Pocket

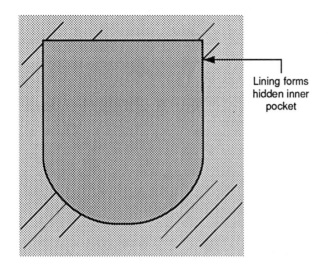

Lining forms hidden inner pocket

Design Analysis:

This pocket looks like an inside-stitched pocket; however, it's actually a lined pocket which is topstitched inconspicuously on the lining itself. To do this, the lining should be lightweight and soft and the pocket/lining seam should be on the edge of the pocket, instead of on the underside.

Pattern Development:

Use the directions for your favorite lined pocket or use the Basic Lined Pocket on page 21.

Sewing Notes:

1. Cut the pocket and lining.

2. Stitch and turn the lining so the pocket/ lining seam is on the pocket edges. Do not press.

 Hint: *The lining can even show a little bit at the edges.*

3. Right sides up, pin the pocket to the garment. Place the pins toward the center of the pocket instead of at the edges.

4. Carefully roll the edges of the pocket back to expose the lining. Set the pocket, stitching only on the lining.

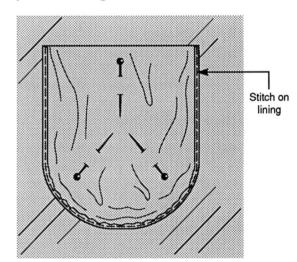

Stitch on lining

5. Right sides up, press the pocket lightly so it covers the lining and stitching line.

Magic-Lined Patch Pocket

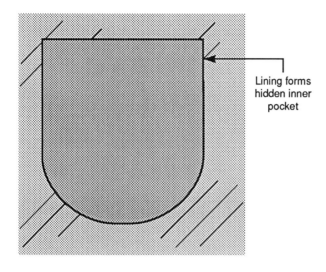

Lining forms hidden inner pocket

Design Analysis:

This sturdy patch pocket will withstand more use and abuse than most patch pockets. And once you've made a couple, you'll decide it's just as easy as your old methods.

On this pocket, the pocket and lining are not sewn together. Instead, the lining is sewn to the garment to create an inner pocket. Then, the pocket itself is sewn over it. With this unusual application, you can create a durable pocket which will not sag or bag.

Pattern Development:

Use the pattern for a Basic Lined Pocket (page 21).

Sewing Notes:

1. Cut one pocket and one pocket lining. Snip the foldline on the pocket. Cut a piece of interfacing the size and shape of the finished pocket. Sew or fuse it to the wrong side of the pocket.

2. Machine stitch around three sides of the pocket 1/2" from the raw edges.

 Hint: *For curved corners, ease baste or crimp 1/4" from the edge. For square corners, miter the corners to reduce bulk.*

3. Right sides together, join the tops of the pocket and lining. Do not leave an opening for turning.

4. Press the pocket/lining seam toward the lining. Press the hem to the wrong side at the clips. Open flat again. Then press the 5/8" pocket seam allowances to the wrong side.

5. Trim and grade the seam allowances as needed for the fabric. On bulky fabrics, notch the curves so they will be smooth and flat.

6. Wrong sides together, fold the pocket on the foldline.

7. Right sides up, position the pocket on the garment. Using two pins near the top of the pocket, pin the pocket in place.

8. Lift the bottom of the pocket and pin the lining to the garment. Remove the pins on the outside of the pocket near the foldline and unfold the pocket so it is upside-down. Pin the top of the lining in place.

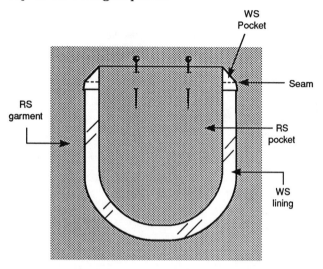

9. Using a disappearing marking pen, draw a stitching line on the lining 1" from the edges. Taper the line at the foldline to 3/4".

10. Using a short straight stitch, stitch on the marked line.

> **Hints:** *If you begin and end the stitching 1/8" below the opening, the upper corners will be easier to shape.*
>
> *On square pockets, stitch lower corners of the lining with curves so the pocket won't collect lint in the corners.*

11. For a neater finish on the inside of the pocket, press the lining seam allowance toward the wrong side of the lining. Then trim the seam allowance.

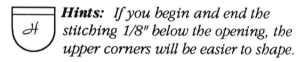

> **Hint:** *When speed sewing, trim the lining close to the stitched line, leaving a little extra on the hem allowance. Clip*

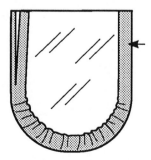

the hem allowance at each end of the foldline so the upper corners will be easy to shape. Stitch over the raw edge of the lining with a zigzag stitch (W,2; L,2).

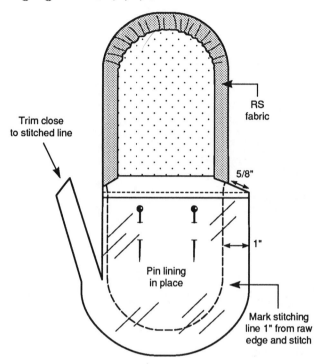

12. Fold the pocket into place. Edgestitch or topstitch the pocket, or hand stitch with a running stitch from the wrong side.

> **Hint:** *Nancy Zieman uses invisible thread and stitches with a machine blind-hem stitch around the edge of the pocket. This positions the straight stitches on the garment, while the zigzag stitches catch the pocket.*

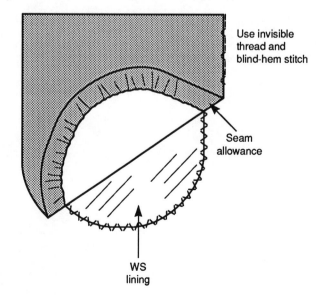

Round Pocket With Button

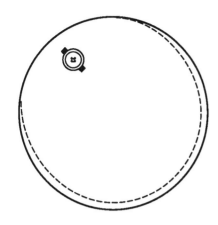

Design Analysis:

When this pocket is set, a large section—approximately one quarter to one third the total circumference—is left unstitched to form the opening. Attractively lined with self-fabric or a companion fabric which shows at the opening, the pocket opening can button to the garment or form a cuff.

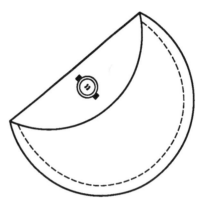

Pattern Development:

Use a compass to outline the pocket. The diameter of the pocket should be the finished pocket size plus 1/2" (two 1/4" seam allowances).

Sewing Notes:

1. For each pocket, cut two pocket sections.

2. Right sides together, stitch around the circles with a 1/4" seam.

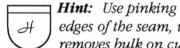 ***Hint:*** *Use pinking shears to trim the edges of the seam, which automatically removes bulk on curves.*

3. Make a small slash near the bottom of the pocket lining. Turn the pocket right-side-out. Press so the seam is exactly at the edge and close the slash.

4. Make a buttonhole on the edge opposite the slash.

Hint: *Locate the buttonhole perpendicular to the edge and 3/4" to 1" from it. If the design calls for buttoning the cuff to the pocket, stitch the buttonhole with the lining side up.*

5. Right sides up, pin the pocket on the garment and stitch, leaving an opening for the hand. Backtack at each side of the opening.

6. Mark the button location on the garment and sew on the button. Or sew the button on the pocket and fold the opening down to form a cuff. Or eliminate the buttonhole completely and anchor the cuff with a short swing tack to keep it from flapping.

3. Novelty Pockets

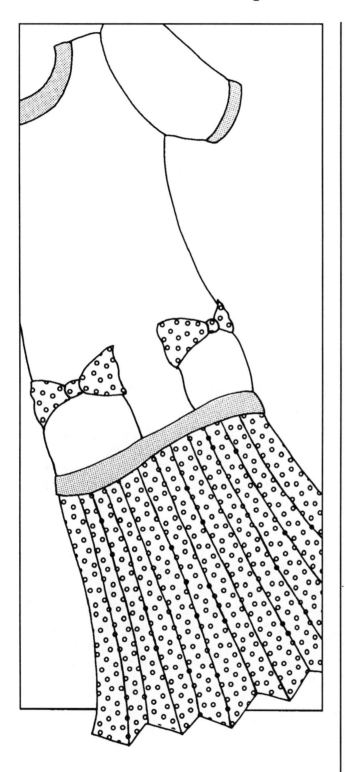

The Basic Unlined Pocket (page 2) or Flat-Lined Pocket (page 26) is frequently used as jumping off points for designing novelty pockets.

Here's where you can let your imagination loose—pleat or tuck bands or pockets, add seams and piping, play with color blocking. See the Designer's Worksheet on page 109 to help you plan.

Be sure to read the General Directions starting on page 91 for instructions on interfacings, finishes, and setting techniques.

Inside-Stitched Pocket

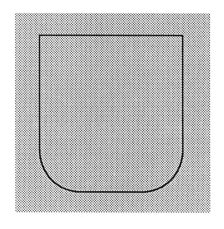

Design Analysis:

Frequently used on expensive sport jackets for men and women, the Inside-Stitched Pocket is durable. It is the most difficult patch pocket to make and in the fashion industry, it is one of the most expensive.

Hint: If this is your first Inside-Stitched Pocket, choose a medium-sized or large pocket pattern with broadly rounded corners. Apply the pocket to the garment section before assembling the garment and plan your design for only one pocket, instead of for a pair.

The Inside-Stitched Pocket can be unlined or flat-lined (see page 26). It is set by stitching on the inside of the pocket and frequently has no visible stitching on the outside of the pocket.

Pattern Development:

Use the pattern for an Unlined (page 2) or Flat-Lined (page 26) Pocket. Trim the seam allowances to 3/8".

Sewing Notes— Method One:

This industrial method, which Miss Giuntini taught me when I was at Laney College, is my favorite.

1. Cut a pocket from the fashion fabric. Trim seam allowances to 3/8".

2. Using short clips, mark the raw edges of the pocket with these matchpoints. First fold the pocket in half vertically and mark the bottom at the center. Mark the sides just above the curves. Then mark the curves in two or three places.

3. Make a cardboard template the finished size of the pocket.

4. Place the template on the pocket and carefully transfer the matchpoints on the pocket to the template.

Pocket

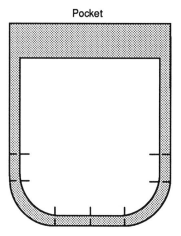

5. With the garment section right side up, chalk around the template and mark the matchpoints. Remove the template. Draw another line 3/8" inside the traced line. Carefully transfer the matchpoints to the inside line.

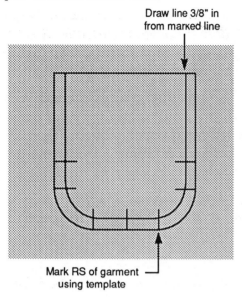

Draw line 3/8" in from marked line

Mark RS of garment using template

6. Stitch around the pocket 1/4" from the edges, crimping the curves. The hem should be edge-finished, folded, and pressed in place.

7. Right side down, place the pocket on the garment to the left of the traced pocket. Match the raw edge of the pocket to the inside line on the garment. Begin at the upper right corner of the pocket and stitch a 1/4" seam around, keying the matchpoints as you go and pulling the pocket around to match the tracing. Yes, you are actually stitching *inside* the pocket!

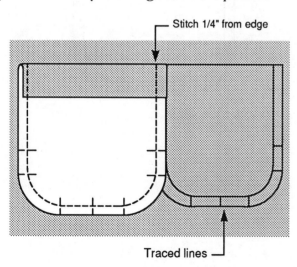

Stitch 1/4" from edge

Traced lines

Hints: *Atlanta retailer **Liz Mann**, uses a zipper foot to stitch easily. I like a straight-stitch foot.*

If the matchpoints don't match at the center of the bottom, rip back to the last notch that matches and restitch.

Even though the original seam allowance was 3/8", stitch only 1/4". Some fabric will be lost in the turn-of-the-cloth and the pocket should fit to the garment smoothly without pulling.

8. Fold the *corners* of the seam allowance down into a triangle and reinforce them by hand. Work with the garment wrong-side-up and make a series of catchstitches in the hem area parallel to the stitching line. Sew through the garment, seam allowances, and pocket hem without catching the outer layer of the pocket.

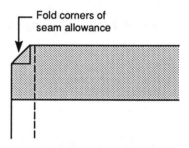

Fold corners of seam allowance

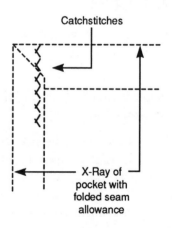

Catchstitches

X-Ray of pocket with folded seam allowance

9. Leave the pocket plain or pickstitch 1/4" around the pocket 1/4" in from the edge. Cover the pocket with a press cloth and press lightly.

Many men's jackets are topstitched 1/4" from the edge. Trim the seam allowance to a skinny 1/4" before topstitching to enclose the raw edges between the two stitched lines.

Sewing Notes—
Method Two:

This is a modification of the home-sew method recommended by many teachers. I've always disliked it because the pocket is frequently too tight and causes the garment section underneath to wrinkle, but in this modification, you'll find a couple of hints to prevent that problem.

1. Make an Unlined (page 2) or Flat-Lined (page 26) Pocket.

2. Using a cardboard template the finished size of the pocket, lightly press the seam allowances to the wrong side.

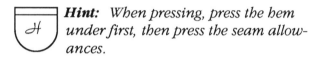 *Hint:* When pressing, press the hem under first, then press the seam allowances.

3. Right sides up, position and pin the pocket on the garment.

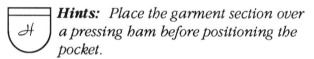 *Hints:* Place the garment section over a pressing ham before positioning the pocket.

Place the pins at right angles to the edge, pinheads towards pocket, and about 1/4" away.

4. Set the machine for a wide, long zigzag stitch (W,4-L,4), loosen the tension, and stitch around the pocket, barely catching the pocket edge.

5. With a regular straight stitch or a crooked straight stitch (W,.5-L,2), stitch around inside the pocket. Do not reset the tension.

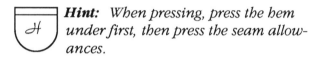 *Hint:* Begin at the upper left corner (as you're looking at the pocket) and stitch 3/8" to 1/2" from the raw edge, using a zipper or straight-stitch foot.

6. Examine the finished pocket. If it's too taut, rip out the inside stitching and try again. If it has more lip at the edge than you like, stitch again farther from the raw edge and closer to the fold.

7. Remove the zigzag basting. Secure the upper corners and press the pocket.

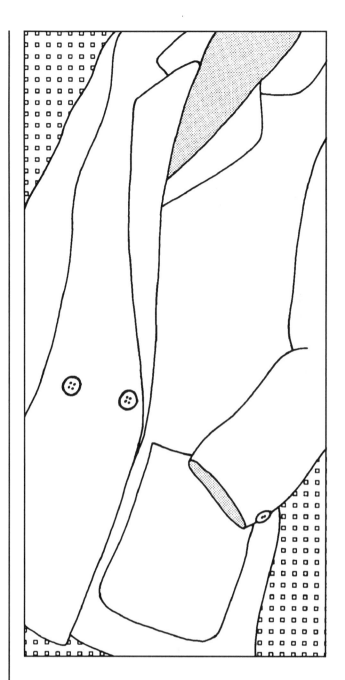

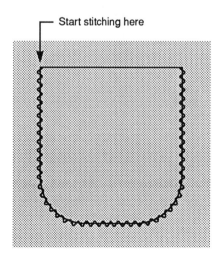

Start stitching here

Variation: Square Inside-Stitched Pocket

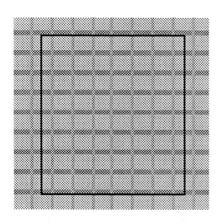

Design Analysis:

Square Inside-Stitched Pockets are much more difficult to sew than pockets with round corners, but on some garments, such as coats, the finished result is worth the effort.

In these directions, the sides are machine-stitched; then the bottom is finished by hand.

Pattern Development:

Use the pattern for an Unlined (page 2) or Flat-Lined (page 26) Pocket. Trim the seam allowances to 3/8".

Sewing Notes:

1. Complete the pocket and mark the bottom at the center.

2. Mark the pocket location and guidelines on the garment section.

3. Right sides together, key the upper right corner of the pocket with the inside marked line.

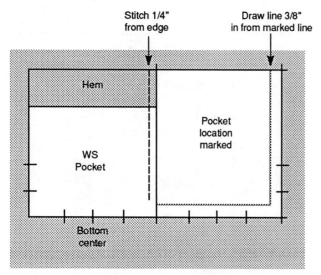

4. Stitch the right side of the pocket 1/4" from the edge, stopping 1/2" from the pocket bottom.

Flip the pocket into position and turn under the seam allowance. Stitch the right side of the pocket (as you look at it) from the inside, 1/4" from the edge, stopping 1/2" from the pocket bottom.

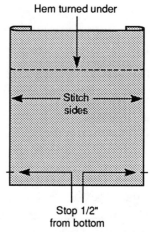

5. Right side up, cover the pocket with a press cloth and press.

6. At the bottom of the pocket, fold under 1/2" (3/8" for heavy or bulky fabrics). Pin or baste the seam allowance in place.

7. Turn the garment wrong-side-up and sew the bottom permanently by hand with a running stitch, short diagonal stitch, catchstitch, or backstitch. Press.

Hint: When choosing the stitch, consider the amount of use or abuse the pocket will endure, as well as your personal preferences. The running stitch is the weakest of the stitches.

Pockets With Cuffs

Sometimes called a self-flap or cut-on flap, the pocket cuff is located at the pocket opening. It can be a cut-on cuff and cut in one with the pocket sections or it can be a separate cuff and seamed to the pocket opening.

Pockets with cuffs can be lined or unlined.

Lined Pocket With Cut-on Cuff

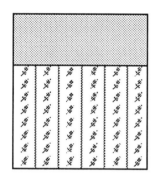

Design Analysis:

In these directions, the cuff you see is actually the lining, while the extra-deep hem of the pocket is folded to the outside of the pocket to form the cuff facing. The cuff can be any depth, but one-third the depth of the finished pocket is a nice proportion.

Pattern Development:

1. Outline the finished pocket and draw the cuff on the pocket outline. For a 5" by 6" pocket, draw the cuff 2" deep. Fold the tracing paper and align with the pocket opening. Trace the cuff.

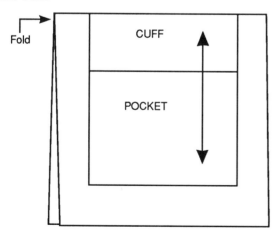

2. Open the paper flat with the cuff above the pocket. Trace the rest of the pocket, indicating the grainline and adding seam allowances all around.

Sewing Notes:

1. For each pocket, cut two pocket sections—one for the pocket and one for the cuff/lining. Mark the foldline at the opening on both sections.

Hint: The pocket will be more attractive if, before stitching, you trim the edges of the pocket 1/8" in the cuff area and the edges of the lining 1/8" in the pocket area.

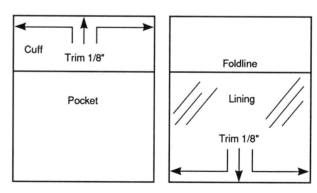

2. Wrong sides together, seam all edges of the pocket, leaving a 1-1/2" opening on the side toward center front or at the center bottom.

3. Trim all seams to 1/4", except at the opening.

4. Turn the pocket right side out, sew the opening closed if desired, and press. Fold the flap into the finished position and press the foldline lightly.

Hint: Generally, when this opening is toward the garment center, it won't be noticeable if it's left open. You can also place the opening at the bottom. If you close it with slipstitching, do not pull the stitches tight and it will remain inconspicuous.

5. Topstitch around the cuff 1/4" from the edges, lining side up. Begin and end the topstitching on the pocket about 1/2" below the foldline.

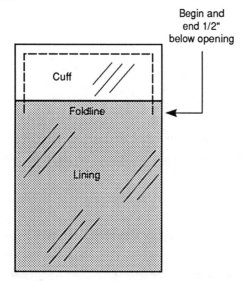

Begin and end 1/2" below opening

Cuff

Foldline

Lining

6. Set the pocket to the garment, stitching from the foldline 1/4" from the edges and holding the cuff out of the stitching area.

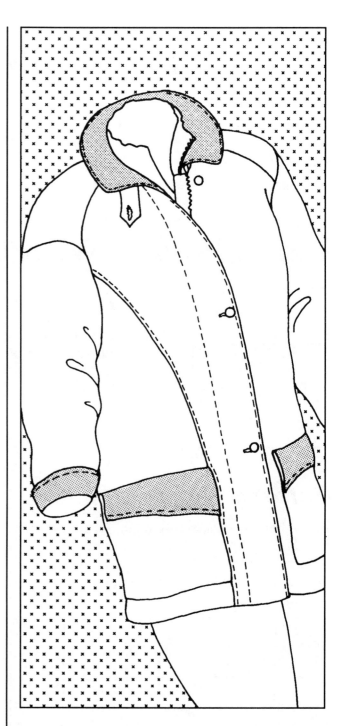

Unlined Pocket With Cut-on Cuff

Design Analysis:

Cut with a contrast cuff, this unlined pocket features a shaped cuff. It is first assembled like a pocket with a faced opening. Then it is applied to the garment so that a portion of the faced area can fold down to make the cuff. The flap can also be self-fabric. This design is unsuitable for bulky fabrics.

Pattern Development:

1. *Pocket pattern:* Outline the finished pocket. Draw the cuff on the pocket outline. Fold the tracing paper forward at the opening, and trace the cuff.

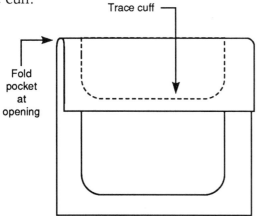

2. Open the paper flat. Add seam allowances to all edges. Indicate the grainline.

3. *Cuff pattern:* For the cuff hem, use a red pencil to draw a line on the original paper pocket 1-1/2" below the pocket opening. Trace the cutting lines around the top of the pattern. Indicate the grainline.

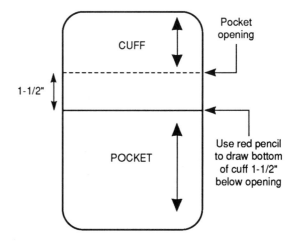

Sewing Notes:

1. Cut out one pocket/cuff facing and one cuff. Mark the openings on both sections.

2. Interface the cuff and pocket as needed.

3. Finish the raw edge of the pocket cuff hem. Trim the sides of the cuff 1/8" below the opening.

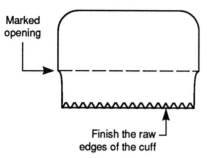

Marked opening →

Finish the raw — edges of the cuff

4. Trim the raw edges around the top of the pocket 1/8", beginning and ending at the opening and tapering out to the foldline.

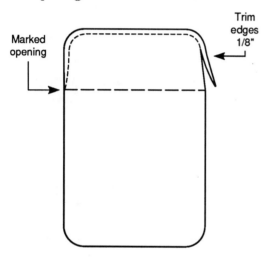

Marked opening →

Trim edges 1/8" ←

5. Right sides together, match and pin the cut edges of the cuff and pocket, and stitch a 1/2" seam. Grade appropriately.

6. Turn the pocket cuff right sides out. Press. Then press the pocket seam allowances under. Fold the flap into the finished position and press lightly.

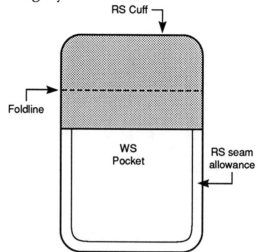

RS Cuff →

Foldline →

WS Pocket

RS seam allowance ←

7. Leave the flap plain or topstitch to correspond with other details on the garment.

8. Set the pocket to the garment, beginning and ending at the top of the flap.

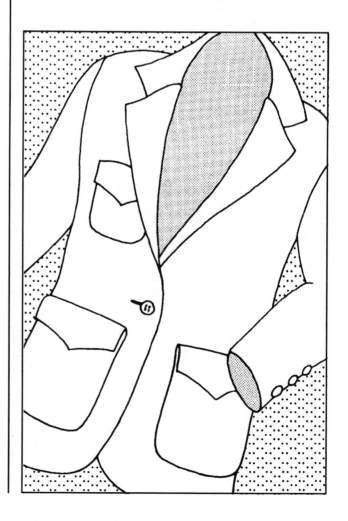

Unlined Pocket With One-Piece Cuff

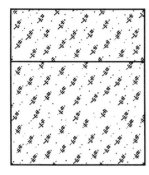

Design Analysis:

Cut all-in-one piece, this unlined pocket features a self-fabric cuff. It is first assembled like a pocket with a very deep hem. Then it is applied to the garment so that a portion of the hemmed area can fold down to make the cuff. The cuff can be any depth, but one third the depth of the finished pocket is a nice proportion.

This design is unsuitable for bulky fabrics and the lower edge of the cuff must be straight.

Pattern Development:

1. Outline the finished pocket. Draw the cuff on the pocket outline. For a 5" by 6" pocket, draw the cuff 2" deep. Fold a piece of tracing paper like the finished pocket—first forward at the pocket opening, then back up at the bottom of the cuff. Trace the cuff.

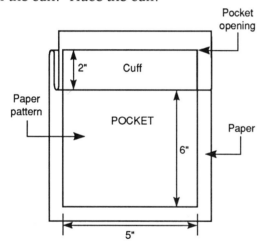

2. Open the paper flat. Align the bottom fold on your tracing paper with the pocket opening. Trace the rest of the pocket. Connect the sides of the pocket and cuff. Add a 1-1/4" hem allowance and 5/8" side and bottom seam allowances. Indicate the grainline.

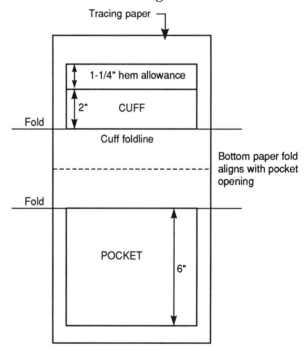

Sewing Notes:

1. Cut out one pocket. Mark the foldline at the bottom of the cuff with snips.

2. Finish the raw edge of the pocket hem allowance (see page 99).

3. Right sides together, fold the pocket at the points marked in Step 1. Stitch the sides and grade appropriately.

4. Turn the pocket cuff right side out. Press. Then press the seam allowances to the wrong side.

5. Fold the cuff into the finished position and press lightly. Do this before stitching the hem so it won't pull. By hand or machine stitch the hem to the pocket.

6. Leave the cuff plain or topstitch to correspond with other details on the garment.

7. Set the pocket to the garment, beginning and ending at the top of the pocket.

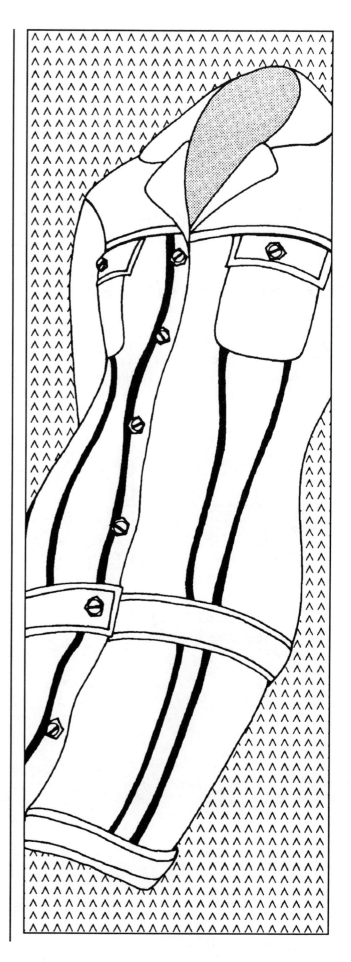

Pockets With Tucks

Tucks can be used singly, in pairs or clusters, or all over. They can be vertical, horizontal, or on the bias. Pockets with tucks can be asymmetrical or symmetrical.

Technically, a tuck is a fold of fabric stitched in place, usually on the outside of the design. And, since all tucked designs have only two elements—tucks and spaces—the how-to of patternmaking is a simple process: start with the spaces and simply add the amount to be stitched out for the tucks.

These directions for making tucks can be applied to any garment or garment section, including skirts, blouses, sleeves, jackets, baby dresses, and, of course, pockets.

The design possibilities are endless, since the tuck width, the space between the tucks, the tuck style, and the arrangement of the tucks can be varied.

Here are few ideas I've seen on ready-made designs: A bias-cut pocket with overlapping tucks on the lengthwise grain, cross tucks, a group of pintucks on two adjacent sides, notched tucks, graduated tucks, pintucks, corded tucks, tucked stripes to make a solid, stitched down tucks, clustered tucks, and reverse tucks.

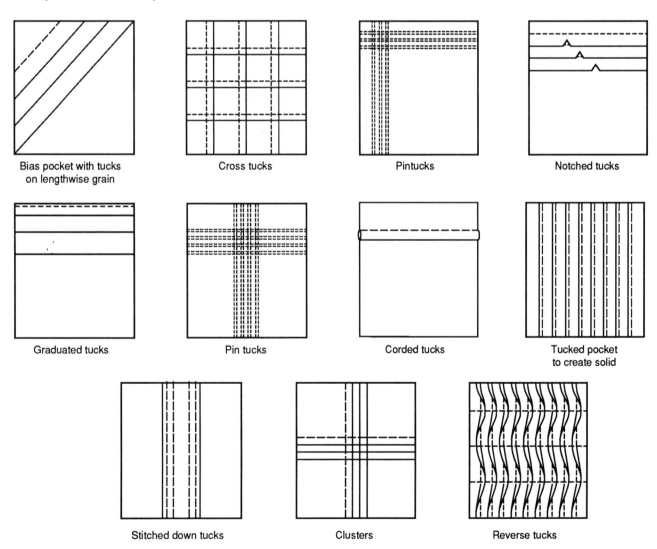

Bias pocket with tucks on lengthwise grain

Cross tucks

Pintucks

Notched tucks

Graduated tucks

Pin tucks

Corded tucks

Tucked pocket to create solid

Stitched down tucks

Clusters

Reverse tucks

Tuck Terminology

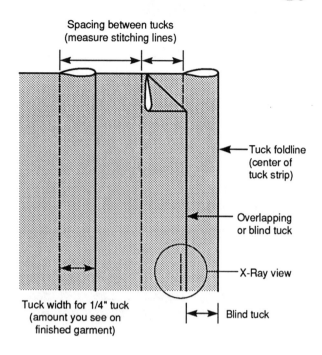

Spacing between tucks
(measure stitching lines)

Tuck foldline
(center of
tuck strip)

Overlapping
or blind tuck

X-Ray view

Tuck width for 1/4" tuck
(amount you see on
finished garment)

Blind tuck

Tuck width is width of tuck that shows.
Tuck strip is twice tuck width.
Tuck foldline is center of tuck strip.
Tuck spacing is distance between stitching
   lines.
A *pintuck* is a tuck 1/16" to 1/8" wide.
A *crosstuck* is a vertical and horizontal tuck.
A *blind tuck* has the stitching covered by an
   adjacent tuck.

Pocket With Pintucks

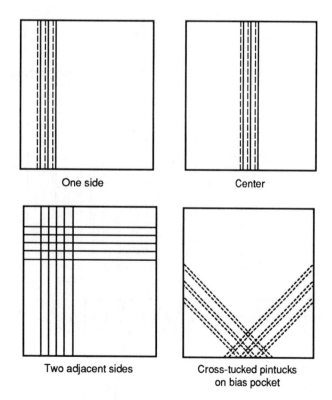

One side

Center

Two adjacent sides

Cross-tucked pintucks
on bias pocket

*On this pocket, very small tucks—1/16"
to 1/8" wide—are used in groups or an
all-over pattern. Some ideas include a
pintuck group at one side or at the center,
groups on two adjacent sides, cross-tucked
pintucks, and crosstucked pintucks on a
bias pocket.*

*Generally, it's better to tuck the fabric
first; then cut out the pocket.*

*To make a pintuck, fold the fabric
wrong sides together. Edgestitch, using the
inside of the regular presser foot or an
edgestitch foot as a guide. If you prefer a
wider pintuck, stitch a skinny 1/8" from
the edge.*

*You can also make pintucks with a
pintuck foot and twin needles. With this
method, you don't fold the fabric. Try
tightening top tension to make more
pronounced pintucks.*

Easy Tucked Pocket

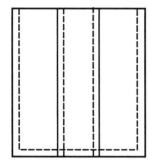

Design Analysis:

This easy tucked pocket features two 1/4"-wide tucks at the center that are spaced 1/2" apart. Although the pocket can be lined or unlined, these directions are for an edge-to-edge lining.

Pattern Development:

1. Outline the finished pocket. When the pocket is finished, this area will be divided into spaces or fabric areas between the tucks. The finished pocket will not get larger or smaller, no matter how many tucks are added. In these directions, the pocket is 5" wide by 6" long, but it can be any size you choose.

2. Make the pattern for an Edge-to-Edge Lining (see page 27). Trace the outline for the finished pocket, indicate the grainline, and add 5/8" seam allowances to all edges.

3. On the original outline, draw two vertical lines for 1/4"-wide tucks at the pocket center, spacing them 1/2" apart.

Hint: I draw the pocket center with a light blue pencil, and the tuck stitching lines with a dark blue pencil.

4. Using a red pencil, draw a horizontal guideline 1" below and parallel to the pocket opening. Number the vertical pattern sections 1-2-3 from left to right.

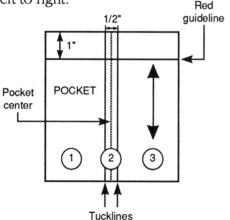

5. On another piece of paper 4" longer than the pocket, make a tuck strip for each tuck. For each tuck, the tuck strip will be *twice the tuck width plus 1/8"* (turn-of-the-cloth loss). For a 1/4"-wide tuck, the distance between the two lines is 5/8". Use the dark blue pencil to draw two parallel lines this distance apart. Use a regular pencil to draw the tuck foldline midway between the two. Use the red pencil to draw a perpendicular guideline about 2" from the top of the tuck strip. Repeat to make a tuck strip for second tuck.

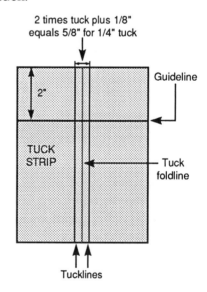

Hint: Since a tuck has two folds, one at the edge and one at the stitching line, a small amount of fabric will be lost in the turn of the cloth. This amount will range from 1/8" to 1/4", depending on the fabric weight and bulk.

6. Cut the pocket pattern apart on the tuck lines (dark blue). Place the pocket on the tuck strip so

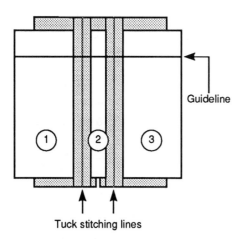

Guideline

Tuck stitching lines

that the blue and red lines are aligned between sections 1 and 2. Tape. Repeat for each tuck.

7. Since this pocket is lined, add seam allowances to all edges. If it is unlined, add a 1" hem allowance at the top.

8. Trim away the excess paper.

 Hint: If the pocket is shaped, fold the tucks in place before trimming to true the edges.

Sewing Notes:

1. Cut one pocket and one pocket lining.

2. Mark all tuck foldlines at the top and bottom with a small V-shaped notch. Mark the stitching lines with 1/8" snips.

3. Wrong sides together, fold the first tuck on the foldline. Stitch the tuck. Repeat for all tucks. Press.

Hint: Stitch so the needle thread will show on the finished pocket. On one side of the pocket, stitch the tuck from top to bottom and on the other, stitch from bottom to top.

4. Line the pocket.

5. Set the pocket to the garment.

Hint: Topstitching 1/4" from the edge is particularly attractive on this design; however, since the lining will then show, it should be self-fabric or an attractive contrast fabric.

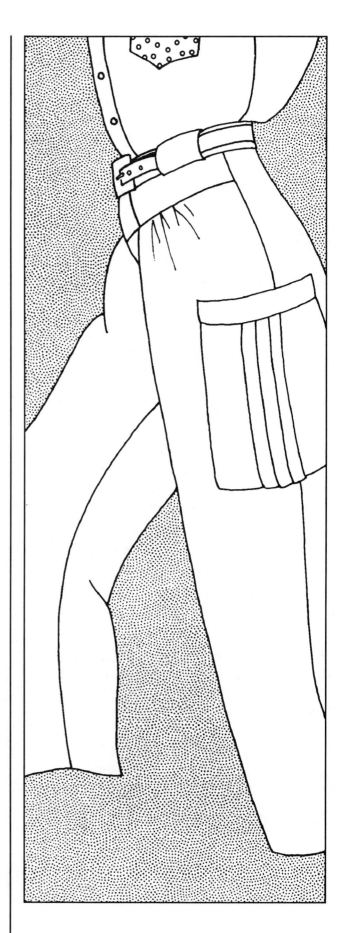

Pocket With Overlapping Tucks

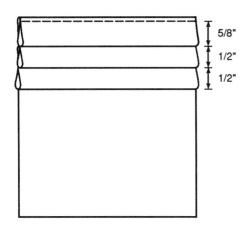

Design Analysis:

Unlike most tucks which have a visible stitching line, overlapping or blind tucks are located so that the folded edge of one tuck overlaps the stitching line of the next tuck. Generally, overlapped tucks are not used as frequently on pockets or garments because they add bulk and require additional fabric.

This unlined pocket features three horizontal tucks near the pocket opening, which look like a cuff. Each tuck is 3/4" wide and each space is 5/8", making the tucks overlap 1/8".

Pattern Development:

1. Outline the finished pocket. Use a dark blue pencil to draw the tuck stitching lines, spacing them 5/8" apart. Locate the first stitching line 1/8" below the pocket foldline. Draw the two remaining stitching lines parallel to the opening, spacing them 5/8" apart.

2. For each tuck, make a tuck strip 1-5/8" wide (see page 51).

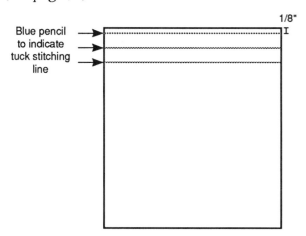

3. Tape the tuck strips to the pocket pattern.

4. For an unlined pocket add a 1-1/4" hem allowance. Add seam allowances and indicate the grainline.

Sewing Notes:

1. Cut one pocket from the fashion fabric.

2. Finish the raw edge of the hem allowance.

3. Mark the ends of the tuck foldlines with small V-shaped notches. Mark the stitching lines with 1/8" snips.

4. Wrong sides together, fold bottom tuck on the foldline. Stitch the tuck. Repeat for all tucks. Press tucks down.

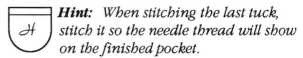

Hint: *When stitching the last tuck, stitch it so the needle thread will show on the finished pocket.*

5. Complete the pocket and set the pocket to the garment.

Pocket With Cross Tucks

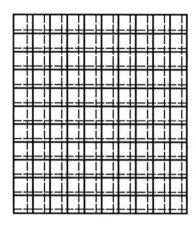

Design Analysis:

When you put a lot of tucking on a fabric, it tends to shrink. Therefore, for best results when using multiple tucks, I tuck the fabric first. Then I use a regular pocket pattern to cut out the pocket. To do this you need two paper patterns—one for cutting the untucked fabric and one for cutting the tucked fabric.

This lined pocket features 1/4"-wide tucks spaced 1/2" apart. On a pocket 5" wide by 6" long, there are nine vertical rows and eleven horizontal rows.

Pattern Development:

1. *Tucked pocket pattern:* First make the pocket pattern which you'll use for cutting the tucked fabric. Outline the finished pocket. Draw the tuck foldlines with a regular pencil. Later you'll use this to position your finished pocket exactly.

To plan the tuck spacing, add the tuck width to the amount you want to show on the finished pocket. On this design, the spacing between tucks is 1/2", which equals 1/4" (the tuck width) plus 1/4" (the space which will show between). Draw the tuck foldlines on the pattern, starting 1/2" from the top and side edges and spaced every 1/2".

Indicate the grainline and add 1-1/2" seam allowance to all sides.

2. *Untucked pocket pattern:* Now make the pattern which you'll use to cut the untucked fabric.

First measure the width of the finished pocket outlined in Step 1. Multiply the number of tucks by the amount of fabric to be stitched out, which is twice the finished tuck size. Add this to the finished width. Add 3" for seam allowances, 1-1/2" on each side. Repeat for the pocket length.

For the untucked pocket pattern, cut a rectangle using these minimum measurements.

Let me show you how this works for this design:

To determine the width:
The pocket is 5" wide.
Each tuck is 1/4" wide. The amount required for each tuck is (2 x 1/4") or 1/2".
There are nine vertical tucks. The amount added for each seam allowance is 1-1/2".
Minimum width: 5" + (9 x 1/2") + (2 x 1-1/2") = 12-1/2"
To determine the length:
Minimum length: 6" + (11 x 1/2") + 3" = 14-1/2"

Hint: *Now that you know how to plan this pocket mathematically, you may choose to select a striped or plaid fabric that plans itself.*

Sewing Notes:

1. Cut one pocket from the fashion fabric, using the pattern for the untucked pocket. Cut one lining from self-fabric or lining material, using the pattern for the tucked pocket.

2. First draw a line with a temporary marking pen 1-1/2" from the left side on the lengthwise grain. This is the seam allowance. To mark the first vertical tuck, draw the tuck foldline 1/4" away. To make the next vertical tuck, draw the tuck foldline 3/4" away—the tuck width of 1/4" plus the 1/2" space between stitching lines. Snip all the foldlines in the seam allowances. If you mark and stitch one tuck at a time, you may distort the fabric and your tucks will look crooked.

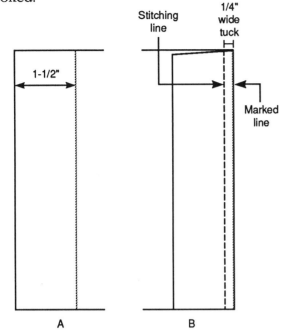

3. Mark the first horizontal tuck about 2" from the top. Mark the next horizontal tuck foldline 3/4" away. Continue marking foldlines every 3/4". Snip all the foldlines in the seam allowances. If you have planned this properly, you'll have no extra tucks in the seam allowance.

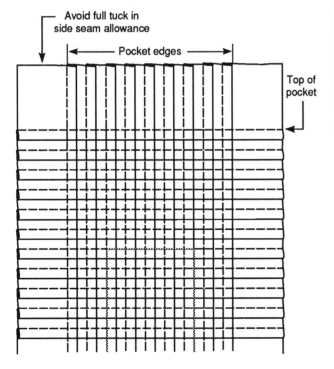

 Hint: *You can't avoid having the tuck ends in the seam allowances, but you don't want a full tuck which will add unnecessary bulk.*

4. Press along all vertical foldlines, then all horizontal foldlines. Be sure to use the same thread on the needle and bobbin. Stitch all tucks 1/4" wide. On the vertical tucks, you'll see the needle thread; on the horizontal tucks, you'll see the bobbin thread.

5. Right side up, place the pattern for the tucked pocket on the tucked material. Adjust the pattern so the tucks are centered under the pattern. Pin. Cut out the pocket.

Hint: *Fold the seam allowances of the pattern up so you can position the pattern easily. Pin the center of the pocket in place and unfold the seam allowance. Then cut.*

6. Complete the lined pocket and set it to the garment.

Hint: *If this pocket won't be functional, sew it on by hand.*

Tucked Stripes

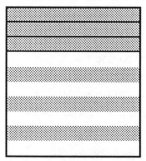

Tucks at top

Design Analysis:

On this pocket design, a striped fabric is tucked to form a solid block of color. The entire pocket can be tucked or just one section—i.e., top or center.

The tuck width, which is determined by the desired effect, and the width and pattern of the stripes, can be the full width of a stripe or a fraction of it.

On this square pocket, the stripes are cut on the bias. At the center, three tucks form a solid block of color.

Stitch here ↓

Tucks center

Reverse Tucks

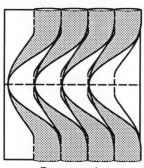

Reverse tucks

Design Analysis:

This novelty pocket can be made with solid-colored fabrics, but it is particularly interesting when an even stripe is used. First, the entire pocket is tucked and all tucks are pressed in the same direction. Then a row of stitching is made over the tucks, pushing them in the opposite direction. The space between tucks cannot be closer than 1/4" and the twists cannot be closer than 2" or the fabric will distort.

Pocket With Notched Tucks

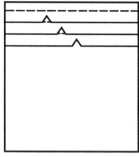

Notched tucks

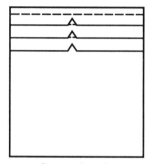

Centered notch

Design Analysis:

This interesting design came from author Shirley Smith. The pocket has three 3/4"-wide tucks, spaced 3/4" apart. Each tuck has a notch at the folded edge. The notches are generally more attractive when they are the same or less than the tuck width.

On this design, the notch on the center tuck is located at the middle of the pocket and the tucks at the top and bottom are 1" away; however, all notches can be centered.

This design is particularly attractive when a pair of pockets is used on a blouse front and the notches are staggered to form the side of a "V".

The pocket can be lined or unlined.

Pattern Development:

1. Outline the finished pocket. Indicate the grainline.

Use a dark blue pencil to draw the tuck stitching lines. Begin 3/4" below the pocket opening. Space the lines 3/4" apart.

Using a red pencil, draw a guide line on one side perpendicular to the tucks. (See page 51.)

Number the sections from top to bottom.

2. Make three tuck strips 1-5/8" wide ([2 x 3/4"] + 1/8") apart. Using the red pencil, draw a perpendicular guideline about 2" from one end of each strip.

3. Cut the pocket apart and tape it to the tuck strips. (See page 52.)

4. Add seam and hem allowances.

Sewing Notes:

1. Cut one pocket and, if the pocket is lined, cut one pocket lining.

2. Mark the fold and stitching lines for the tucks.

3. To stitch the notches, begin right sides together. Fold and pin the tucks in place. Using a temporary pen, on the top tuck, make a dot on the tuck foldline 1" to the left of the pocket center. On the middle tuck, make a dot at the pocket center. On the bottom tuck, make a dot 1" from the other side of the center. Snip the dots.

Using a temporary marking pen, draw the stitching lines for the notch. I begin and end at the folded edge 3/8" from the snip so the widest part of the notch equals the tuck width. The notch can be narrower, but I wouldn't make it wider. Make the notch 5/8" high at the center.

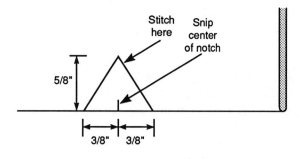

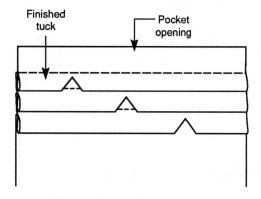

4. Using a short stitch length, stitch the notches. Trim close to stitching and clip to highest point of notch.

5. Unpin the tucks, turn them right-side-out, and press. Repin the tucks wrong sides together. Stitch and press.

6. Complete the pocket and set it to the garment.

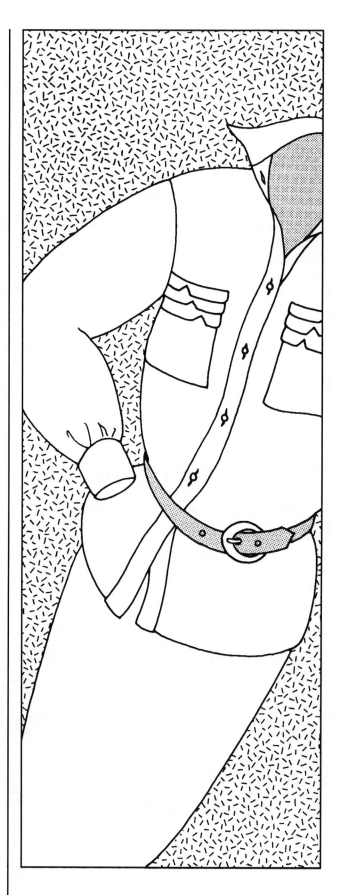

Pleated Pockets

Frequently used on sportswear, pockets can have one or more pleats. Pleats can be used singly, in pairs, or in clusters; and they can be located at the center, to one side, or diagonally.

A pleat is a fold of fabric laid back to form an underlay on the wrong side of the garment or garment section. Pleats can be formed in several ways, but on pockets, they are usually folded and pressed. Some, such as box pleats, are stitched, while others, such as knife pleats, are left unstitched. A few, such as inverted pleats, can be either unstitched or partially stitched.

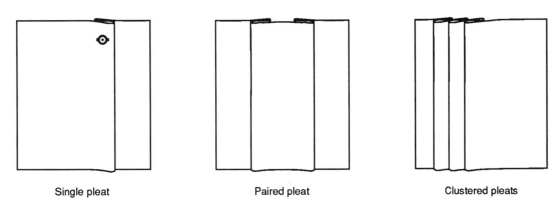

Single pleat   Paired pleat   Clustered pleats

Types of Pleats

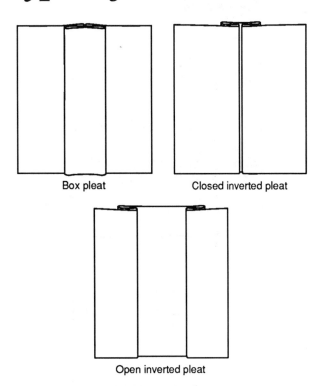

Box pleat

Closed inverted pleat

Open inverted pleat

Although there are many types of pleats, only three—knife, inverted, and box—are popular on pockets. The knife pleats have one outside fold and one inside fold. On pockets, they are sometimes used singly, but they are generally used in pairs to form inverted or box pleats.

Simply described, the box pleat is two knife pleats facing in opposite directions. On pockets the box pleat is frequently stitched to hold its shape. The inverted pleat is two knife pleats facing each other. When the outside folds meet, it is called a closed inverted pleat; when they don't, it's called an open inverted pleat. If you're thinking ahead, you've probably already guessed that when you have a box pleat on one side of the fabric, you have an inverted pleat on the reverse.

In many respects pleats and tucks are similar. The primary differences are (1) the tuck fold is usually on the outside of the garment, while the pleat fold is on the inside; and (2) tucks are stitched and pleats are not. Even so, neither is true all the time.

These differences don't seem as noticeable in garment construction as in patternmaking. When adding a tuck, insert the tuck strip at the stitching line; when adding a pleat, insert the underlay strip at the outside fold.

Pleat Terminology

The pleat depth is the distance between the outside fold and the inside fold. The pleat underlay is the full amount of the pleat unseen from the right side of the garment; it is twice the pleat depth. The space is the distance between the outside folded edges of two pleats.

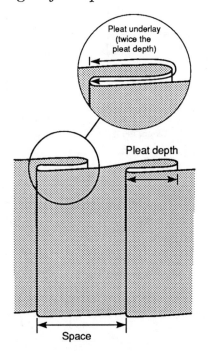

Pleat underlay (twice the pleat depth)

Pleat depth

Space

Pocket With Inverted Pleat

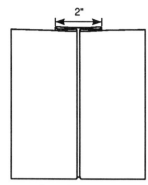

Design Analysis:

An inverted pleat has two knife pleats turned toward each other so the outside folds meet. Although this pocket can be unlined, it is frequently finished with an edge-to-edge lining.

These pockets are particularly attractive on crisp fabrics, sportswear, and safari jackets where they are often called cargo pockets. They can be large or small depending on the garment and the pocket locations. Since the pleat tends to be bulky at the top, many pockets are finished with a band (see page 10) or with a separate flap set above the pocket.

These directions feature an inverted pleat at center. The total pleat depth is 2".

Pattern Development:

1. *Pocket pattern:* Outline the finished pocket. Indicate the grainline and add seam allowances to all edges.

2. *Lining pattern:* Before proceeding, make the lining pattern. Trace the cutting lines of the pocket pattern and indicate the grainline.

3. On the pocket pattern, draw the center of the pleat. Number the sections 1 and 2. Use a red pencil to indicate a matchpoint on the pleat about 1" below the opening.

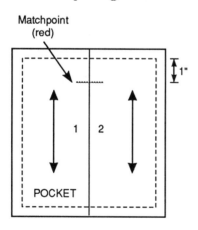

4. Make the pleat underlay on another piece of paper 2" longer than the pocket and about 6" wide. Since the inverted pleat is 2" deep, the underlay is 4" wide—twice that amount. Draw five parallel lines spaced 1" apart. Label the lines A, B, C, D, E. Using a red pencil draw a guideline perpendicular to the lines and about 2" below the top of the paper.

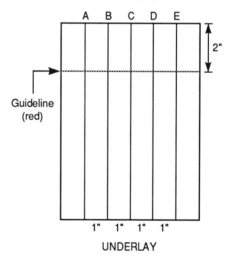

5. Cut the pocket on the pleat line. Align and tape the edges of the pocket sections with the outside lines on the underlay so that the red matchpoints are aligned.

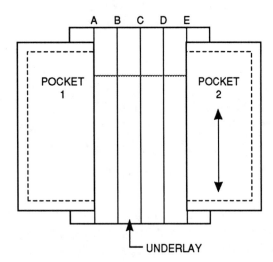

Align matchpoints

6. Wrong sides together, fold along A and E. Bring them together to the front at C. Now trim away the excess paper at top and bottom.

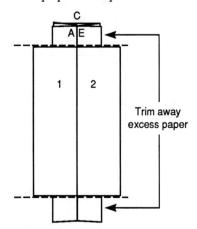

7. Make a clean pattern.

Hint: *You'll probably skip this step, but it is easier to use patterns which aren't composed of lots of odds and ends taped together.*

Sewing Notes:

1. Cut one pocket and one pocket lining. Mark the tops and bottoms of the outside folds (lines A and E) with small notches. Mark the center of the pleat underlay with clips.

2. Right sides together, fold the pocket at the center clips. Beginning at the notches, machine stitch the top of the pocket for 7/8" (the seam allowance plus 1/4"). Backstitch. Repeat at the bottom.

Hint: *The pleat will be easier to press if you baste the entire pleat in place.*

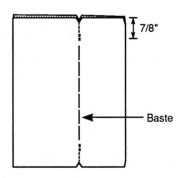

3. Wrong side up, align the clips at the center with the notches and press the pleat into position. Remove the basting.

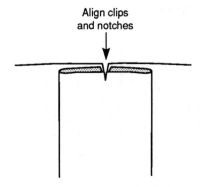

Align clips and notches

4. Complete the lined pocket.

5. Edgestitch the pocket to the garment and, if desired, stitch again 1/4" from the edge.

Pocket With Inverted Pleat (Separate Underlay)

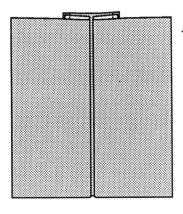

Design Analysis:

At first glance, this variation of the Inverted Pleat frequently looks the same. But instead of being a one-piece pocket, this design has two side pocket sections and a separate underlay. It is frequently used when the fabric is wiry or difficult to press because the seamlines will lie flatter than foldlines; however, it can be used to create a novelty pocket with the underlay a different color, different grain, or even a different fabric.

Pattern Development:

Using the preceding directions on page 61 through Step 5, cut the underlay on lines B and D. Add seam allowances and matchpoints to the cut edges and indicate the grainline on the new underlay pattern.

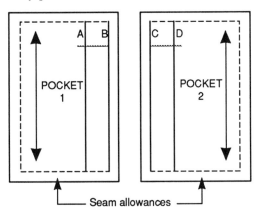

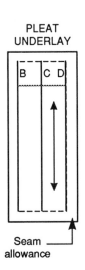

Sewing Notes:

1. Cut two pocket sections and one underlay. Cut one lining. Mark the top and bottom of the pleat foldlines with small notches.

2. Right sides together, match and stitch the long sides of the underlay to the pocket sections.

3. Press the underlay seams flat. Do not press them open. Wrong sides together, fold the pleats at the notches and press.

4. Machine baste the top and bottom of the pleat just inside the seamline for 7/8". (See Step 2 on page 62.)

5. Line the pocket and set it to the garment.

Pocket With Box Pleat

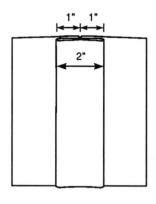

Design Analysis:

A box pleat is an inverted pleat wrong-side-out. If you already have a pocket pattern for an inverted pleat, you can use it instead of making a new pattern. Pockets generally have only one box pleat located at the center, but it can be off-center.

Most box pleats are designed so that each pleat depth is one half the outside pleat and the folds meet on the wrong side. For example, each pleat depth for a 2"-wide box pleat is 1". However, if the pleat depth is less than one-half the total pleat, the folds won't meet; if the pleat depth is greater, the folds will overlap.

Functional pockets are generally unlined so the pocket will expand to accommodate bulkier items. But when a pocket is lined, the lining can be cut either by a separate lining pattern the size of the finished pocket, like the inverted pleat design on page 61, or it can be cut by the pocket pattern. If it's cut by a separate lining pattern, the lining will hold the pleat in the pleated position; if it's cut using the pocket pattern, the pleat will be lined, allowing the pocket to expand when used.

These directions are for an unlined pocket with one 2"-wide box pleat located at the pocket center. The depth of each side of the pleat is 1".

Pattern Development:

1. Outline the finished pocket. Use a blue pencil to draw the pleat—two parallel lines equidistant from the center. For these directions, draw each line 1" from the center. These are the pleat style lines. Use a red pencil to draw a guideline parallel to the opening and about 1" below it.

Indicate the grainline, number the three pocket sections, and label the style lines A and B.

Hint: *Always label sections from left to right. Pocket patterns can usually be made without numbering the sections, but it's a good habit to develop so that when you apply these patternmaking skills to other sections of the garment, your patterns will be perfect.*

2. Analyze the design: On this pocket, the box pleat is 2" wide and each pleat depth is 1". This allows the inside folds to meet.

Hint: *When fabric economy is important, reduce the pleat depth to 1/4". For a pocket with greater expansion, increase the depth to 2".*

3. On a separate piece of paper at least 3" longer than the pocket, make a pleat underlay *for each pleat*. Using a blue pencil, draw three parallel lines, spacing them 1" (the pleat depth) apart. Repeat on a second piece of paper.

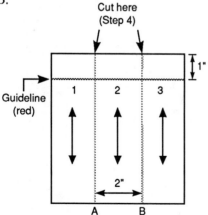

Cut here
(Step 4)

Guideline
(red)

1"

1   2   3

2"

A   B

Using a red pencil, draw a guideline perpendicular to the lines and about 2" below the top.

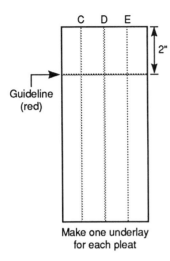

Guideline (red)

Make one underlay for each pleat

4. Cut the pattern apart on the pleat style lines (A and B) you drew in Step 1. For each pleat, match the cut edge on the pocket to the outer lines on the underlays. Align the red guidelines and tape the sections. You will have three pocket sections and two pleat underlays.

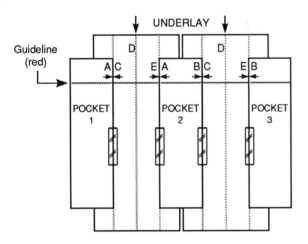

Guideline (red)

UNDERLAY

POCKET 1   POCKET 2   POCKET 3

5. Fold the pleats into position by folding the lines on either side of the center front wrong-sides-together. On this design, the inside folds meet. Trim off excess paper.

Hint: Cut several more patterns. Experiment with deeper pleats which overlap and shallower pleats which don't meet.

6. Trace the pattern from Step 5 onto another piece of tracing paper. Add a 1-1/4" hem at the top and 5/8" seam allowances on the sides and bottom. Trim away the excess paper.

Hint: Since this pocket is a simple rectangle, you can add the seam and hem allowances before folding the pleat if you use a large piece of paper at the beginning; however, if the pocket were shaped, the underlay wouldn't fit properly. You would need to fold the pleat, trim the excess paper, open flat, and then add hem and seam allowances and refold to check it.

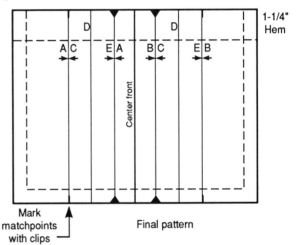

1-1/4" Hem

Center front

Mark matchpoints with clips

Final pattern

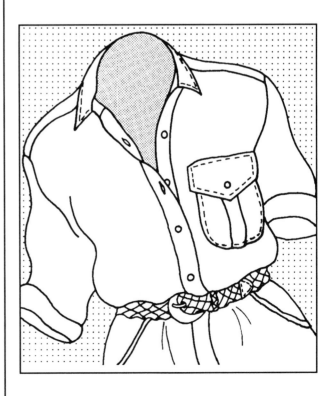

Sewing Notes:

1. Cut one pocket. Mark the top and bottom of the outside pleat folds (EA and BC) with small notches. Mark the corresponding matchpoints— the other side of the underlays (AC and EB)— with clips.

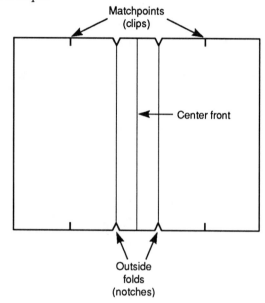

Matchpoints (clips)

Center front

Outside folds (notches)

2. *When the inside folds meet,* this is the easiest way to work:

Wrong sides together, fold the pocket in half, matching the notches. Beginning 2" (the width of the box pleat) from the folded edge, stitch 1-1/2". Backtack. Repeat at the bottom notches, stitching 3/4".

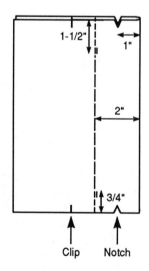

1-1/2"   1"

2"

3/4"

Clip   Notch

Machine baste the section between. Open the pocket and adjust the pleat so it is centered over the stitching. Press. Remove basting.

Hint: *The center section can also be left machine-stitched, but the pocket won't expand.*

When the pleats are very deep or shallow, this method works well:

Right side up, fold one side of the pleat at the notches wrong sides together. Match the notches to the clips on the underlay. Baste as needed and press. Repeat for the other side of the pleat.

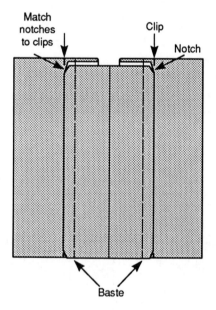

Match notches to clips

Clip

Notch

Baste

3. Trim out the extra fabric in the pleats in the bottom seam allowance and hem.

4. Complete the pocket and set it to the garment.

Pleated Pocket With Band

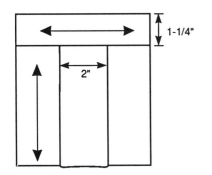

Design Analysis:

This pocket combines two basic patternmaking techniques—the pleat (inverted or box) and the band (page 10). The pocket can be lined or unlined.

In these directions, the pocket has a 2"-wide pleat at the center and a 1-1/4" band.

Pattern Development:

1. Outline the finished pocket. Draw the band (1-1/4" wide) at the top of the pattern. Indicate a matchpoint on the band/pocket seamline.

2. Indicate the grainlines. The grainline on the pocket usually duplicates the grain on the garment section, while the grainline on the band is usually perpendicular to the pocket grain. This is especially attractive on stripes.

3. Cut the pattern apart on the band/pocket seamline.

4. To make the lower pocket pattern, add seam allowances to all edges and add the box pleat (see Patch Pocket With Box Pleat on page 64).

 Hint: *If the pocket has a lining, the lining pattern can be traced before the pleat is added or traced afterwards.*

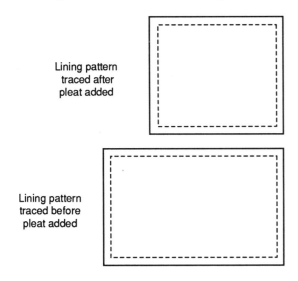

Lining pattern traced after pleat added

Lining pattern traced before pleat added

5. To make the band pattern, position the fold on tracing paper on the band foldline. Add seam allowances to the remaining three edges of the band. Turn the tracing paper over and trace the cutting lines to make the band facing.

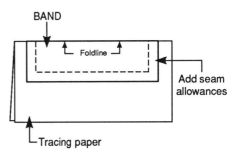

Sewing Notes:

Review the Sewing Notes for Pocket With Box Pleat on page 65 and Unlined Pocket With Band on page 11.

Banded Pocket With Flared Pleat

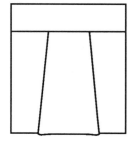

Design Analysis:

This pocket features a flared box pleat with seams at the inside folds. The flared pleat is designed to be wider at the bottom than at the top. Since the pleat folds are offgrain, they cannot be pressed crisply on any but lightweight fabric.

In these directions, the pleat is 2" wide at the top and 3" wide at the bottom. The pleat depth is 1" and the pocket has an edge-to-edge lining (see page 28).

Pattern Development:

1. Outline the finished pocket *without the band* and draw the style lines of the pleat on it with a blue pencil (A and B). For these directions, begin each line at the band/pocket seamline 1" from the center and end 1-1/2" from the center at the bottom. Use a red pencil to draw a guideline near the top.

Indicate the grainline and number the three pocket sections.

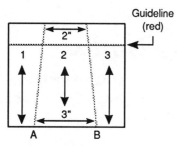

2. Before continuing, make the lining pattern. Trace the finished pocket pattern *without the band* and add seam allowances to all edges.

3. On separate pieces of paper longer and wider than the pocket, make four pleat underlays. For each underlay, use a blue pencil to draw two parallel lines, spacing them 1" apart (the pleat depth). Leave some paper on each side of the blue lines for ease in aligning, taping, and marking seam allowances. Make a guideline 2" from the top.

4. Cut the pattern apart on the pleat style lines (A and B). Match and tape each pocket edge to one of the underlays.

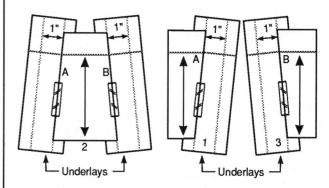

5. *Pocket sides pattern:* Extend the top and bottom lines to the parallel line on the underlay. Fold along the A or B style line and trim excess paper above, below, and on the outside blue underlay line. Open out flat. Lay pattern on a new piece of tracing paper and trace. Add seam allowances to all edges.

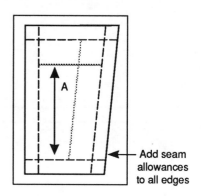

6. *Center section pattern:* Fold the pleats in place along A and B style lines. With the paper folded, trim along the top and bottom of the pattern and the outside blue lines. Then open the paper and add seam allowances to all edges.

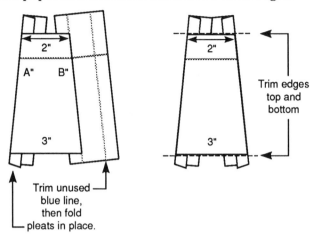

Trim edges top and bottom

Trim unused blue line, then fold pleats in place.

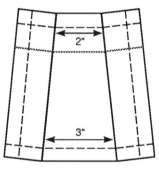

Open paper and add seam allowances to all edges

7. Pin the paper pattern together, pleats folded in place. Turn it over, wrong-side-up, and draw matchpoints near the bottom.

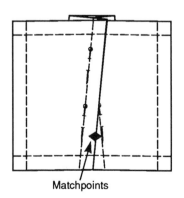

Matchpoints

Sewing Notes:

1. Cut two side sections and one center section. Cut one lining. Mark the top and bottom of the pleat style lines with small notches. Mark the matchpoints (from Step 7 above) on the side sections.

2. Right sides together, match and pin the center section to one of the side pockets. Stitch. Repeat for the other side.

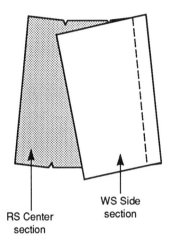

RS Center section

WS Side section

3. Press the pocket seams flat, not open. Wrong sides together, fold the center section at the notches, aligning the matchpoints on the side sections, and press the pleat style lines. If desired, edgestitch the edges of the pleat, holding the side sections away from the stitching.

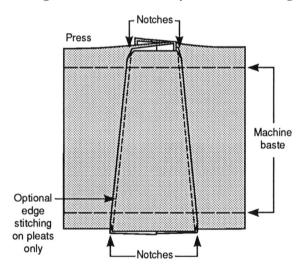

Notches

Press

Machine baste

Optional edge stitching on pleats only

Notches

4. Machine baste the pleat in place with a row of stitching just inside the seamline across the top and bottom.

5. Line the pocket. Complete the band at the top (see page 11). Set the pocket to the garment.

Variation: Pleated Pocket With Shaped Band

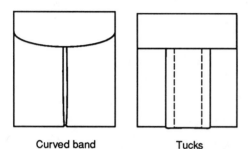

Curved band   Tucks

Be imaginative: Bands can be curved, as well as V-shaped or straight. Pleats can be off-center, eliminated completely, replaced by one or more pleats of a different type, or replaced by tucks.

Generally the band width is approximately one-quarter the pocket depth.

Variation: Pleated Pocket With Flap

Flaps are frequently used with box pleats and inverted pleats to cover the bulk at the top of the pocket. The pocket flap is at least 1/4" wider than the pocket. See Chapter 4, Flaps, page 85, for construction information.

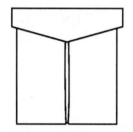

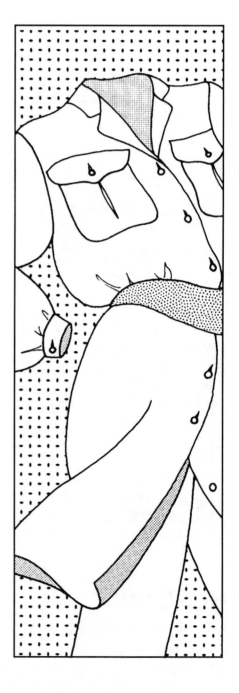

Bellows Pockets

Sometimes called a military or expanding pocket, the bellows pocket has pleated gussets at each side and at the bottom. When empty, the pocket lies almost flat against the garment; when in use, it expands to hold bulky items.

On pockets with straight edges, the gussets are usually cut in one piece with the pocket, but on fancy shapes, the gussets must be cut separately. The separate gusset sections require more fabric; however, if the pattern was made accurately, pockets with separate gussets are usually easier to sew.

Bellows pockets are particularly attractive on active wear and spectator designs and are useful on tennis, golf, photography, hunting, hiking, and fishing outfits.

The bellows pocket can be finished without a fastener at the top, but it will be more secure and attractive if it has a fastener. The most popular finishes are a buttonhole on the pocket with a button on the garment or a flap which buttons to the pocket (see Bellows Pocket With Flap on page 78). Buckles and straps can also be used.

For best results, select a firmly woven fabric which can be pressed crisply. Pockets can be lined, flat-lined, or unlined.

Sewing Notes for Flat-lined Bellows Pocket:

Suitable for fabrics which don't have quite enough firmness for an unlined pocket, the flat-lined pocket is easier to sew than a fully lined one.

1. Using the pattern for the Unlined Bellows Pocket on page 72, make a basic lining.

2. Cut the pocket from the fashion fabric and the lining from lining material.

3. Interface the pocket as needed.

4. Right sides together, join the pocket and lining at upper edge, understitch, and press.

5. Wrong sides together, press the foldline at the opening.

6. Pin the remaining raw edges together. Serge or zigzag to finish them.

7. Complete and set the pocket.

Sewing Notes for Lined Bellows Pocket:

When the fabric is soft or lightweight, a pocket lining will add body, as well as finish the inside of the pocket nicely.

1. Using the pattern for the Unlined Bellows Pocket on page 72, cut the pocket from the fashion fabric and the lining from lining material.

2. Right sides together, stitch the corners of the lining. Repeat for the pocket.

3. Right sides together, join the sides and bottom of the pocket and lining. Press and trim. Begin and end about 1" from the top.

4. Turn the pocket right side out and work the lining smoothly into the pocket corners.

5. At the pocket opening, fold in the seam allowances so the lining is 1/8" below the opening. Slipstitch the opening closed. Press the pocket and pleat foldlines.

6. Set the pocket to the garment.

Unlined One-Piece Bellows Pocket

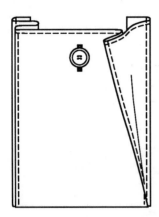

Design Analysis:

This bellows pocket is 6" wide and 8" deep with a 2"-wide gusset and one buttonhole at the top. Although it is described as an unlined pocket, it would be easy to flat-line it (see page 26).

Pattern Development:

1. Outline the finished 6" x 8" pocket on graph paper.

2. To establish the gusset at the sides and bottom, draw two lines parallel to the outside edges and spaced 1" apart. The first line marks the inside fold on the gusset; the second marks the edge which will be sewn to the garment.

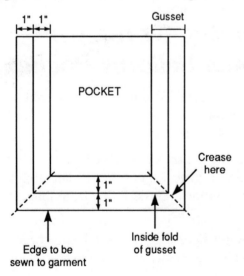

1" 1"

Gusset

POCKET

Crease here

1"

1"

Edge to be sewn to garment

Inside fold of gusset

3. Mark the stitching lines at each corner like a double mitered corner. First, establish a line midway between the bottom and side by creasing the paper pattern at one of the lower corners so that the lines at the bottom and sides match. This makes a 45° angle. At the corner (A), square a line from the creased fold to the inside foldline (B). Then square a line from B to the finished edge of the pocket (C). Fold on the crease and trace the same lines on the other side. The center rectangle you've just made will be cut out later after you add seam allowances.

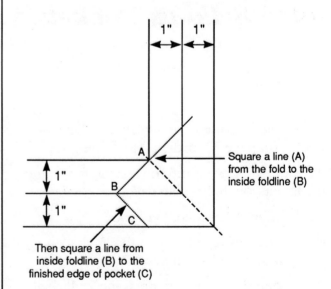

1" 1"

A

1"

B

1"

C

Square a line (A) from the fold to the inside foldline (B)

Then square a line from inside foldline (B) to the finished edge of pocket (C)

Trace the lines you've just drawn onto the opposite corner by folding the paper in half lengthwise and transferring all lines to the opposite corner.

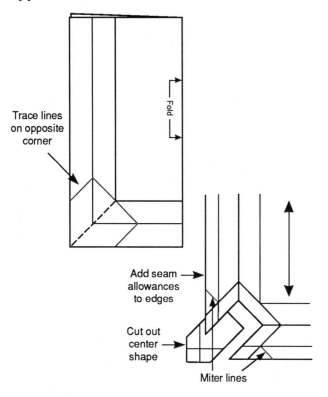

Trace lines on opposite corner

Fold

Add seam allowances to edges

Cut out center shape

Miter lines

4. Add 5/8" seam allowances to all edges, including the opening, and indicate the grainline. Cut out the center rectangle on the cutting lines. At the intersection of the outside foldline and the two seam allowances, draw a line parallel to line BA. This will be the miter line for the seam allowance.

Sewing Notes:

1. For each pocket, cut one pocket from the fashion fabric. To reinforce soft or lightweight fabrics, cut an interfacing for the finished pocket, excluding the gussets. Mark the gusset foldlines with an erasable pen. Mark the miter line on the outside seam allowance.

2. If this is a functional pocket, reinforce the garment section under the pocket. Otherwise, reinforce just the upper corners (see page 105).

3. Make a vertical buttonhole at the pocket center 1-1/2" from the raw edge at the top.

4. Finish the pocket opening with a narrow hem (see page 102).

5. Right sides together, stitch the corners at the bottom to form the boxing. Using a short stitch, begin with a spottack at the folded edge. Stitch to first fold line and pivot. Stitch to the second fold line and pivot. Stitch to the raw edge and spottack. Clip to corner. Press the seams open and trim to 1/4".

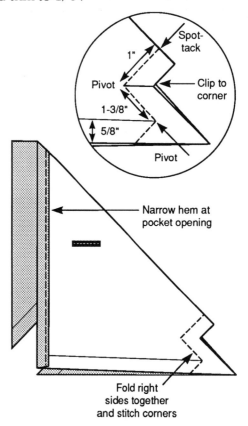

Spot-tack

1"

Pivot

Clip to corner

1-3/8"

5/8"

Pivot

Narrow hem at pocket opening

Fold right sides together and stitch corners

6. Turn the pocket right-side-out.

7. Press the foldlines right sides together to form the pleat. Then press the seam allowances under at the sides and bottom.

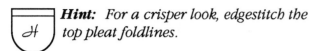 **Hint:** *For a crisper look, edgestitch the top pleat foldlines.*

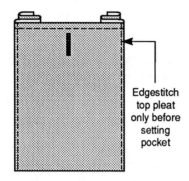

Edgestitch top pleat only before setting pocket

8. Right sides up, pin the center of the pocket to the garment. Hold the pocket out of the way and baste the gusset in place across the sides and bottom. Edgestitch the gusset, without catching the pocket itself. Press lightly.

9. Sew on the button.

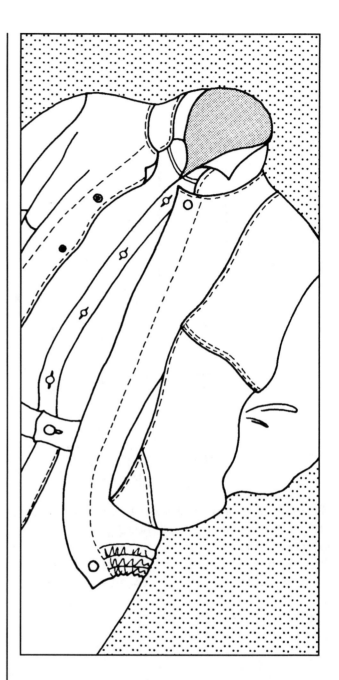 **Hint:** *If you apply the Bellows Pocket to another patch pocket, you can have top entry for the Bellows and side entry for the patch. This is found on many sports clothes.*

Bellows Pocket
With Separate Gusset

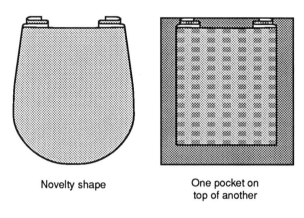

Novelty shape

One pocket on top of another

Design Analysis:

When the bellows pocket has separate gusset sections, the pocket can have a novelty shape; it can look like it is two pockets, one on top of the other; or it can be a novelty design with striped or ribbed fabrics.

This pocket looks like two pockets, one on top of the other. The overall finished size is 7" wide by 8" deep. The "top" pocket is 5" by 7" and the "bottom" pocket is 7" by 8". It has a 1" gusset which is sewn to the top pocket at the outside edge of the gusset and to the bottom pocket on the U-shaped edge of the gusset. Although these directions are for an unlined pocket, it can be lined or flat-lined (see page 26). If you make the striped variation, with all its seams, you will be happier with a lined pocket.

Pattern Development:

1. Outline the finished pocket with the "top" pocket drawn on it. Indicate the grainlines.

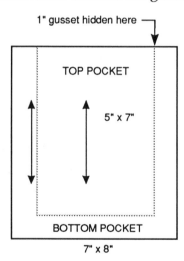

1" gusset hidden here

TOP POCKET

5" x 7"

BOTTOM POCKET

7" x 8"

Hint: *I use a blue pencil to outline the "top" pocket.*

2. *Top pocket pattern:* Trace the "top" pocket on another piece of pattern paper. Add a 1" hem allowance and 5/8" seam allowances to the edges of the "top" pocket.

3. *Gusset pattern:* Use a red pencil to draw the inside edge of the gusset 1-1/4" inside the finished edge of the "top" pocket. Round the

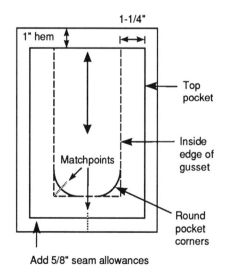

1-1/4"

1" hem

Top pocket

Inside edge of gusset

Matchpoints

Round pocket corners

Add 5/8" seam allowances

inner corners so the pocket will be easier to assemble. Draw matchpoints on the inside curve and at the center of the bottom. Trace the cutting edges of the "top" pocket

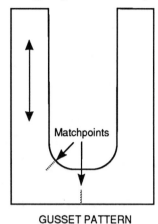

GUSSET PATTERN

pattern including hem allowance and the inside edge of the gusset. Trace the grainline and matchpoints.

4. *Bottom pocket pattern:* On another piece of pattern paper, trace the outside edges of the finished pocket outlined in Step 1. Add a 1" hem allowance and 5/8" seam allowances to the edges. Draw a matchpoint at the center of the bottom. Center the gusset pattern on the bottom pocket pattern, using the matchpoints at the center as a guide. Trace the inside edge along the red pencil line and the matchpoint from the gusset pattern. Indicate the grainline.

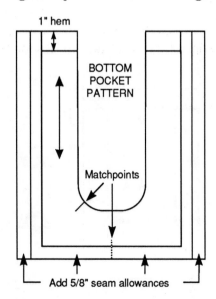

1" hem

BOTTOM POCKET PATTERN

Matchpoints

Add 5/8" seam allowances

Variation for Striped Fabric:

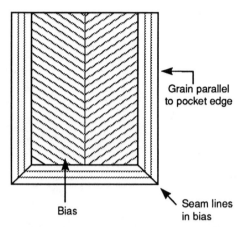

Grain parallel to pocket edge

Bias

Seam lines in bias

1. Fold and cut the "top" pocket in half vertically. Add seam allowances. Draw the grainlines on the two sections so that they chevron. *Generally, the grainlines are on the true bias—a 45° angle from the pocket center, but they don't have to be.*

2. On the "bottom" pocket pattern, add a seamline on the bias at each of the lower corners. Draw the new grainlines parallel to the outside edges.

Sewing Notes:

1. For each pocket, cut the "top" pocket section(s), one gusset, and the "bottom" pocket section(s). (If the pocket is lined, use the original pocket pattern to cut the lining sections.)

2. If you're piecing the "top" sections, right sides together, join the "top" pocket sections.

Top pocket

Then join the outside edges of the "top" pocket and gusset. Trim. Turn right side out. Press.

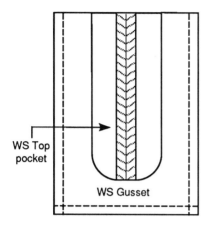

WS Top pocket

WS Gusset

3. Right sides together, join the sections of the "bottom" pocket.

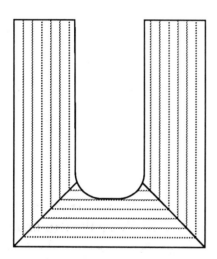

4. Right sides together, join the gusset and "bottom" pocket with a 1/4" seam. Finish the seam and hem edge with serging, zigzagging, or pinking.

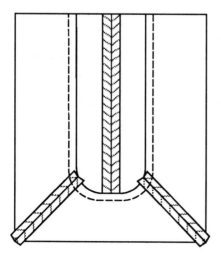

5. Wrong side up, press the hems and outside seam allowances to the wrong side. Tuck in the upper edge of the side seam allowances.

Hints: *For a smoother finish, clip the vertical seams at the opening foldline. Press the seams in the hem in one direction and the seams on the pocket in the other direction.*

*To anchor the hem at the inside edge of the gusset, begin with the pocket **right-side-up**, hold the top pocket out of the way, and ditch-stitch through the gusset and bottom pocket or edgestitch through all layers on the topside.*

Ditch-stitch

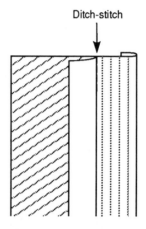

6. Edgestitch the bottom pocket to the garment.

7. To control the pocket at the opening, stitch again through all layers for about 1" parallel to the opening.

Stitch 1"

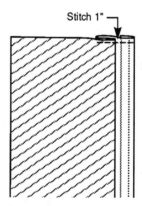

Bellows Pocket With Flap

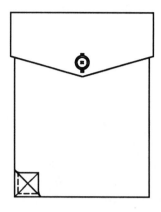

Design Analysis:

This bellows pocket has a flap sewn to the garment just above the pocket. The flap should be 1/4" to 1/2" wider than the pocket.

Pattern Development:

1. Make the Bellows Pocket pattern (see page 72).

2. Make the flap pattern at least 1/4" wider than the finished pocket. For a flat flap, add a 5/8" seam allowance at the top; for a rolled flap, add a 1" seam allowance at the top. (See Flaps on page 85.)

Sewing Notes:

1. Cut out the pocket from the fashion fabric. If desired, cut a lining. For each pocket, cut one flap from the fashion fabric and one flap facing from self-fabric or lining material.

Hint: *On very casual designs, the flap facing is sometimes eliminated and the edges of the flap are finished with a hem. If you plan to use this finish, the flap should have 5/8" seam allowances on all outside edges.*

2. Assemble the pocket (see page 73).

3. Assemble the flap. Trim the flap lining 1/8" on all edges. Right sides together, pin and stitch the edges together, leaving a 2" opening at the top. Trim the seams and turn the flap right side out. Press. If desired, topstitch the sides and bottom. Then make a vertical buttonhole near the point of the flap and centered side-to-side.

4. Edgestitch the pocket in place.

5. Position the flap just above the pocket. Topstitch at the top edge and again 1/4" away.

6. Sew the button on the pocket.

Saddle Bag Pockets

The saddle bag pocket has a front and back which are stitched together to make a pouch. Then the top of the pouch is stitched to the garment or a belt so the pocket hangs free from the garment. The tops of saddle bag pockets can be designed with separate flaps or tabs, flaps cut as part of the pocket back, or straps which loop over a belt.

There are many saddle bag variations; the bellows and porthole pockets are two of the most popular.

Saddle Bag With Flap

Design Analysis:

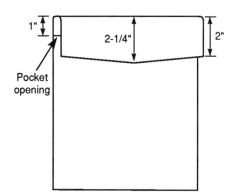

This saddle bag design has three sections: the back, front, and flap facing. Since the pocket back folds to the front to form a flap, the fabric should be attractive on both sides.

Pattern Development:

1. Outline the finished pocket. In these directions the pocket is 8" wide and 9" deep; the flap is 2-1/4" deep; and the flap foldline sits 1" above the pocket opening. Draw the pocket opening. Draw the flap on the front. This will be used as a base for your patterns.

 Hint: *This is less confusing if you use a red pencil to draw the front pocket and a blue one to draw the flap.*

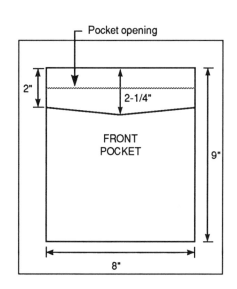

2. *Saddle bag front pattern:* Trace the pocket from the pocket opening down on another piece of pattern paper. Add 5/8" seam allowances on sides and bottom and 1" hem at top. Indicate the grainline.

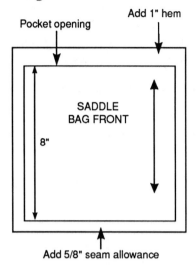

Pocket opening   Add 1" hem

SADDLE
BAG FRONT

8"

Add 5/8" seam allowance

3. *Saddle bag back pattern:* Fold the tracing paper. Align the fold with the top of the saddle bag on the base pattern and trace the flap. Open out the paper. Trace the rest of the pocket. Add 5/8" seam allowances to all edges and indicate the grainline.

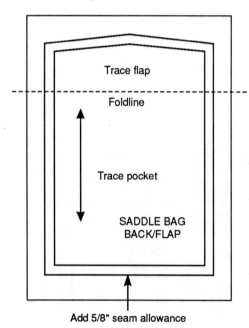

Trace flap

Foldline

Trace pocket

SADDLE BAG
BACK/FLAP

Add 5/8" seam allowance

 Hint: *I use a stiletto tracing wheel when tracing to mark both layers at the same time.*

4. *Flap facing pattern:* Trace the cutting lines of the flap from the base pattern. Add 1-1/2" plus the distance between the top of the saddle bag and the opening of the front pocket (1" on this pocket) to the top of the flap facing. Indicate the grainline.

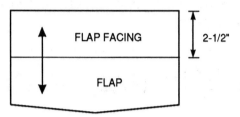

FLAP FACING   2-1/2"

FLAP

Sewing Notes:

1. For each pocket, cut one saddle bag front pocket, one saddle bag back/flap, and one flap facing.

2. On the front pocket, fold under 1/2" twice and stitch.

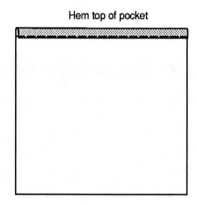

Hem top of pocket

3. Wrong side up, press 1/2" at the bottom of the flap facing to the wrong side. Use a release sheet to fuse a piece of fusible web to the right side of that same seam allowance.

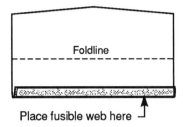

Foldline

Place fusible web here

4. Right sides together, join the pocket front and back at the side and bottom.

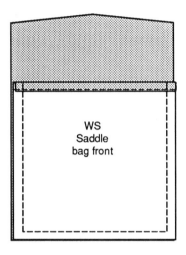

WS
Saddle
bag front

5. Right sides together, join the flap facing and pocket back. The facing should lap over the pocket opening about 1".

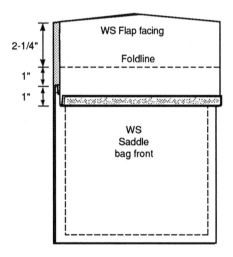

2-1/4"

WS Flap facing

Foldline

1"

1"

WS
Saddle
bag front

6. Trim and grade the seam allowances. Turn the pocket and flap right side out. The bottom of the flap facing will be inside the pocket.

7. Press to fuse the flap facing to the back pocket. Press the foldline at the top of the pocket. Topstitch the flap.

8. Make a vertical buttonhole at the center of the flap, if desired.

9. Position the pocket on the garment. Unfold the flap and stitch at the foldline.

10. Fold the flap into position. Topstitch 1/4" from and parallel to the foldline. The pocket hangs free.

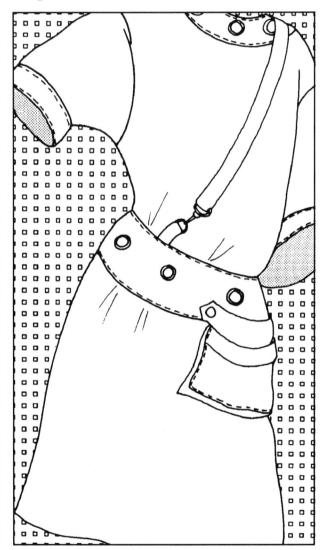

Pocket Patches

Designed for the younger set, these pocket patches can instantly transform a Christmas outfit into a Valentine's Day design, a St. Patrick's Day garment, or just a cute everyday outfit.

The pocket patches can button onto a plain, unlined pocket or button onto the garment itself. They can be either decorative or useful and unlike most pockets, they can be added to a ready-made garment.

In these directions, the patch is 5" by 6".

Easy Lined Patch

Pattern Development:

1. Using your favorite method, make a pattern for a 5" by 6" patch pocket.

2. To make the patch pattern, trace the finished pocket pattern and round all corners. Indicate the grainline and add seam allowances to all edges.

 Hints: *Patches can also be novelty-shaped, such as hearts, Christmas trees, soccer balls, initials.*

To add a patch for a pocket on a ready-made garment, trace the garment's pocket. Then design the patch and add seam allowances.

Sewing Notes:

1. For each pocket, cut one regular pocket and two pocket patches.

2. Decorate one patch with machine embroidery, appliqués, or monograms. You can also use a centered motif from patterned fabric.

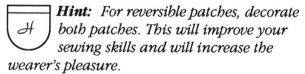 ***Hint:*** *For reversible patches, decorate both patches. This will improve your sewing skills and will increase the wearer's pleasure.*

3. To complete the pocket patches, begin right sides together. Join the two patches, leaving a 2" opening on one side. Trim the seam and turn the patch right side out. Press.

Coax the seam allowances into the opening and close it by edgestitching around the entire patch. Press.

4. Complete the unlined pocket and set it to the garment.

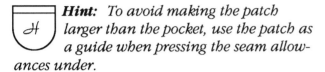 *Hint:* *To avoid making the patch larger than the pocket, use the patch as a guide when pressing the seam allowances under.*

5. Make a buttonhole at each corner of the pocket patch.

6. Center the patch on the garment pocket and mark the button locations. Sew the buttons in place.

7. Button the patch onto the pocket.

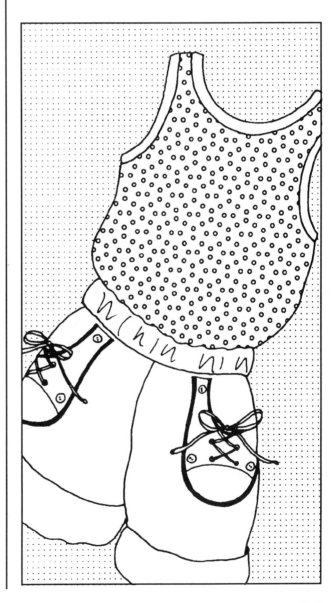

Pocket Patch With Bound Edges

Design Analysis:

This Pocket Patch has round corners and all edges are bound with 1/2"-wide double-fold bias binding.

Pattern Development:

Using the directions for the Easy Lined Patch on page 82, make the pattern for the patch, but do not add seam allowances.

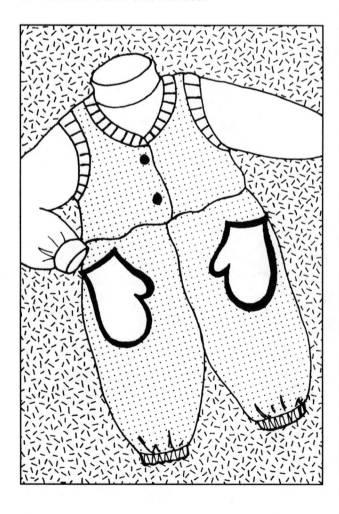

Sewing Notes:

1. For each pocket, cut one regular pocket and two patches.

2. Decorate one patch with appliqué, quilting, or painting. Put in a buttonhole in each corner.

3. Stack the patches so the right sides are out. Stitch around the stack 1/4" from the edge.

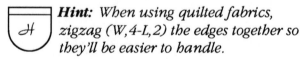 ***Hint:*** *When using quilted fabrics, zigzag (W,4-L,2) the edges together so they'll be easier to handle.*

4. Bind the edges of the patch using your favorite method. Since this is a child's garment, I use a speed finish. Using wide double-fold bias, begin binding on one long side. Slip the patch between the bias layers. Glue-baste.

Then edgestitch or zigzag (W,2-L,2). When you reach the end, fold the bias end under 1/2", overlapping the beginning 1/4".

4. Flaps

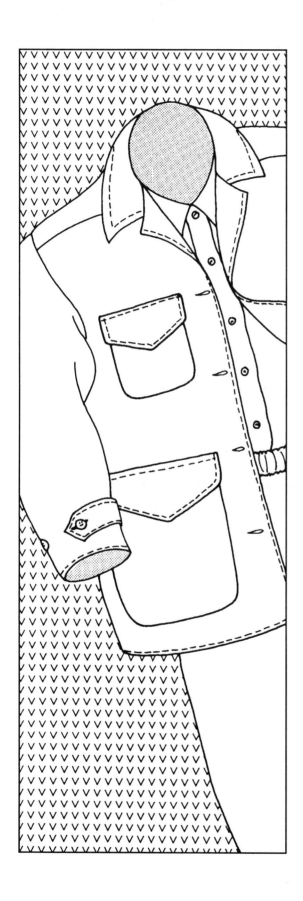

Flaps are applied elements which enhance the garment design. They can be used with almost any patch pocket as either decorative appendages or utilitarian security covers. They are interfaced and assembled using the same criteria and techniques as patch pockets, but unlike pockets, they do not form a pouch, since they are attached only at one edge—usually the upper.

Generally, flaps are located 1/2" above, cover all or part of the pocket opening, and can be straight or shaped. Flaps are usually lined or faced with a traditional lining material, contrast fabric, or self-fabric, depending on the fabric weight and garment design. Occasionally, however, they are hemmed at the free edges.

Usually used in pairs, flaps can be used alone to simulate a slashed pocket or they can be used with patch or inseam pockets. In this book, Patch Pockets With Flaps have the flap applied above the pocket opening; Pockets With Cuffs have the flap applied directly to the front of the pocket openings and don't cover the opening (see page 43).

Like their patch pocket cousins, most flaps duplicate the nap, grainline, and fabric pattern of the garment section. The grain on the flap facing duplicates the grain of the flap. This section focuses on the sewing and patternmaking techniques **which differ from patch pockets.** For in-depth directions for sewing flaps, review the General Directions for Patch Pockets on page 91.

Separate Flaps

These general directions are for separate flaps which can either be applied above patch pockets or faced openings or can be applied as cuffs to the front of the pocket openings.

Pattern Development:

1. Outline the finished flap. It can be any shape—rectangle, pointed, or curved—and it frequently miniaturizes the shape of the collar, lapels, or hemline.

The ends can be parallel to each other but many times the edge nearer the garment center is parallel to the center front while the edge nearer the side seam is parallel to that seamline.

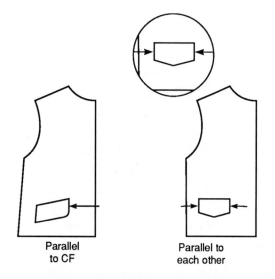

Parallel to CF

Parallel to each other

2. Add seam allowances to all edges.

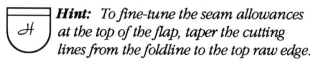

Hint: *To fine-tune the seam allowances at the top of the flap, taper the cutting lines from the foldline to the top raw edge.*

3. Indicate the grainline. It usually duplicates the grainline of the garment section, but it can be on the bias or crossgrain.

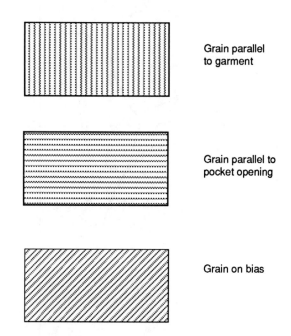

Grain parallel to garment

Grain parallel to pocket opening

Grain on bias

4. If the flap will be sewn into a seamline, indicate a notch on the top edge of the flap. Indicate a corresponding notch on the seamline.

5. If the flap will be sewn to the garment, mark the flap placement line on the pattern or garment section.

Pattern Notes for One-Piece Flap:

When the flap design has straight sides or a straight lower edge, many homesewers prefer to cut a one-piece flap, eliminating some seams and reducing the bulk.

If the sides are straight, eliminate both side seams and add a seam line at the center back of the facing. To sew, fold the flap in half vertically, right sides together. Sew the ends. Press. Then with the seam centered, sew the bottom.

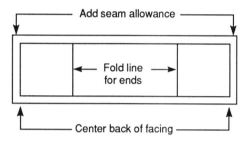

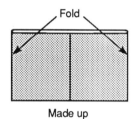

Made up

If the lower edge is straight, cut the flap with a fold at that edge.

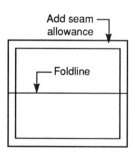

Made up

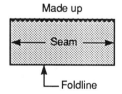

Sewing Notes:

1. When sewing light- to medium-weight fabrics, cut two flaps from the fashion fabric.

When sewing thick or bulky fabrics, cut one flap from the fashion fabric. Cut the flap facing from a lightweight lining material.

Hint: It is frequently easier to sew if the flap is cut on the bias. But a bias-cut flap holds its shape better if the facing is on the lengthwise grain.

When sewing fabrics with patterns, match the fabric pattern on the flap and the garment. If the flap is applied over a dart or seamline, match the end toward the garment center.

Hint: To match patterns easily, cut out the garment section and outline the flap on the section with thread or eraseable marking pen. Lay the flap pattern on the garment section, and trace the fabric design onto the flap pattern. (See page 108.)

2. Interface the flap as needed.

3. Trim all edges of the flap facing 1/8". Right sides together, match and pin the raw edges of the flap and facing together. Stitch.

Hints: Stretch the facing as needed to fit the flap. If the flap has corners, pin a bubble at each corner to control the fullness.

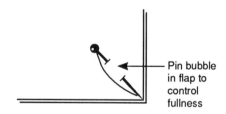

4. To avoid rabbit ears at the corners, shorten the stitch length to 20 stitches/inch (1.75mm) and take two tiny stitches across the corner.

5. Press. Trim and grade the seams. Turn the flap right-side-out.

6. Wrong side up, press the flap so the seamline is visible at the edges.

7. Topstitch, if desired.

8. If the flap will be sewn to a pocket or into a seam or dart, set the flap aside until it's needed.

If it will be sewn directly to the garment, see Flap Applications next.

Flap Applications

These directions are for flaps applied to the garment surface above patch pockets or faced openings. For flaps applied to the front of pockets, see page 78. Following are three flap applications: all-purpose, for lightweight fabrics, and couture.

All-purpose Application

Appropriate for most fabrics, the all-purpose application can be finished in several ways, depending on the garment quality, the fabric, and time available.

1. Fold under the seam allowances at the top of the flap. Pin on the seamline. The facing may peek out just a little.

2. Baste the seam allowances together on the seamline. Then trim the seam allowances to 3/8". Remove any pins and press on the foldline.

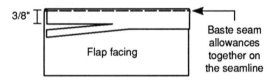

3. Right sides together, position the flap on the garment so the flap is upside-down above the location line. Key the location line and the stitching line on the flap so the raw edges of the flap overlap the line 1/4". Stitch 1/4" from the raw edge. The remaining 1/8" will be lost in the turn-of-the-cloth.

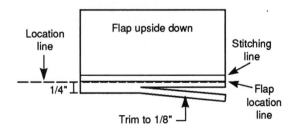

4. Trim the seam another 1/16" – 1/8". Then fold the flap into place and secure it, using one of the methods below.

Topstitch: Particularly appropriate when the garment has topstitching at the edges or on the flap, this method is easy and encloses all raw edges. Topstitch 1/4" to 3/8" from the fold. Secure the ends by pulling them to the back and tying off with an overhand knot.

"Invisible" stitching: Another easy machine method, this application is terrific when you don't want the machine stitching to show. Pin the flap in place. Then at one end, bubble the flap to expose the seamline and flap facing. Beginning at the foldline, machine stitch on the facing for 1/2".

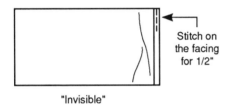

Stitch on the facing for 1/2"

"Invisible"

 Hint: *If you've made the Fake Inside-Stitched Pocket on page 34, you are already familiar with this technique.*

Fell the ends: This hand method is generally used on better garments or on flaps which have lining facings. Beginning at the foldline, hand sew the ends for 1/2", using felling stitches.

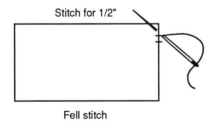

Stitch for 1/2"

Fell stitch

 Hint: *The stitches won't show if you don't pull them too tight.*

Blindstitch: This application is used on better garments when you want an invisible finish. Fold the flap into position and baste about 3/8" below the fold. Turn the garment over and, using the basting as a guide, hand sew through the garment and flap facing with a short running stitch just above the basting. Or, if you prefer working from the right side, lift the flap at the basted line. Use a blindstitch to sew the flap facing and garment.

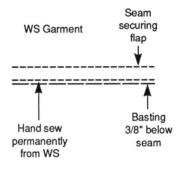

Seam securing flap

WS Garment

Hand sew permanently from WS

Basting 3/8" below seam

or

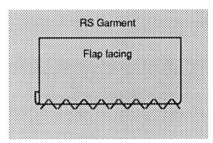

RS Garment

Flap facing

Blindstitch flap to garment

 Hint: *Sew carefully to avoid stitches that show on the right side of the flap.*

5. Remove the basting. Right side up, cover the flap with a press cloth; press lightly.

Application for Lightweight Fabrics

Well-suited for flaps and tabs on shirtings and other lightweight fabric, this application encloses all raw edges. It is too bulky for medium- and heavy-weight fabrics.

For flatter, more attractive flaps and tabs, eliminate the interfacing or use a very lightweight interfacing.

1. Right sides up, position the flap on the garment so the flap is below the location line. Key the raw edge of the flap to the location line.

2. Stitch 1/4" from the raw edge. Trim the seam to 1/8".

3. Fold the flap up at the stitched line so the right side faces the garment. Stitch on the location line, enclosing the raw edges.

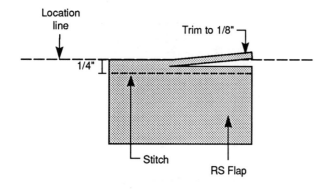

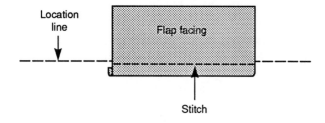

4. Fold the flap into position and press.

Hint: On some wash-and-wear fabrics and blends, the flaps are sometimes unruly and don't lie flat. Use the "invisible" machine stitch or fell stitches (see page 89) at the ends to tame them.

Couture Application

Suitable only for your finest designs, assemble the flap using the couture technique for lining a patch pocket (see page 24). This finishes all edges.

1. Right sides up, position the flap on the garment with the top of the flap aligned with the flap placement line. Baste it in place with a large "X."

2. Secure the upper edge invisibly with a fell stitch or turn the work over and secure it with two rows of short running stitches. Remove basting.

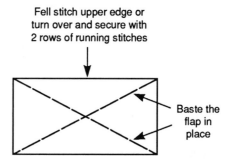

Part II:
General Directions for Patch Pockets

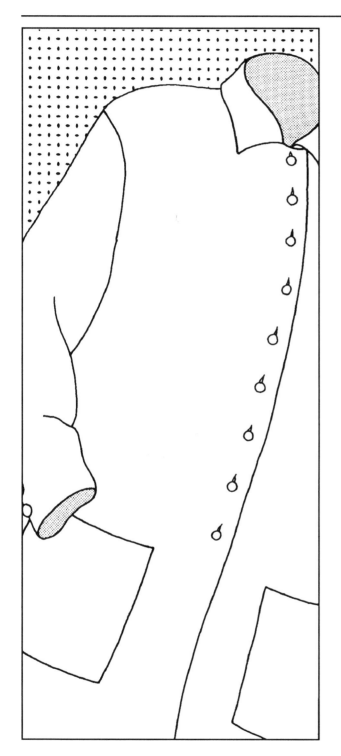

Table of Contents

Pocket Location and Placement 92

The Perfect Location 92

Marking the Pocket Placement 93

Interfacings 94

How to Interface Pockets 94

How to Interface Hems 97

Reinforced Openings 97

Underlining Pockets 98

Finishes for Pocket Openings 99

Traditional Hems 99

Narrow Topstitched Hems 102

Bindings 102

Setting the Pocket 102

General Directions for Applying Patch
Pockets 103

Pressing Techniques 105

Reinforcing the Garment Under the
Pocket 106

Hints for Special Fabrics 107

Plaids 107

Sweater Knits 108

Pocket Location and Placement

Vertically shaped pockets or diagonal placements are more slenderizing than horizontally shaped pockets. When placed at the bust or hipline, pockets add pounds even to the skinniest figures; on skirts, pockets placed close to the side seams add width.

Pocket pairs should be equidistant from the garment center. When placed too far to the side, they add width to the hips; when too high, they broaden the shoulders.

One way to establish the location of the pocket is to subtract the pocket width from the distance between the center front and side seam. Divide the remainder by three and multiply by two. That's how far the front edge of the pocket should be from the center front. If the pocket is 5" wide and the garment section measures 11", the pocket will be 4" from the center front. When placing pockets on a garment for an asymmetrical body, cut one pocket slightly narrower. Apply them an equal distance from the center front.

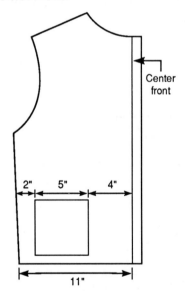

When positioning functional pockets, consider the length of the arm. When the hand enters the pocket, the arm should be comfortably bent. Once inside, you should be able to retrieve items at the bottom without bending over or holding the garment up to reach them.

In *Clear-Cut Pattern Making*, Mary Gorgen Wolfe recommends using your elbow as a guide post. For comfortable, usable pockets, she recommends placing the top of the pocket 2" below the elbow.

When placing pockets at an angle, drop the lower end 1-1/2".

The Perfect Location

It's always easier to sew pockets before the garment is assembled. But if you can't decide where the pockets should be placed before beginning construction, don't despair. Complete the garment, including the hem. Then try the design on and experiment with different locations and different pocket shapes and sizes.

1. Draw several pockets in different sizes and/or shapes. Cut them out and pin them to the garment. If you have enough scraps, cut out the pocket shapes using the fashion fabric. Just ignore the raw edges. Otherwise, use tissue paper.

2. If the garment hasn't been hemmed, pin the hem in place. Then pin the "pockets" in place until you have the look you want.

3. Try on the garment, and examine the pocket shapes and placement while standing in front of a full-length mirror. Move them around and re-evaluate the design.

4. Once you've decided on the pocket design and location, remove the garment before unpinning the pocket(s).

5. Mark the location of the two upper corners with pins. If the fabric will be marred by pins, use fine needles or chalk, or place the pins under the finished pocket.

6. When the design has paired pockets, use the placement of the first pocket as a guide when marking the other pocket. Wrong sides together, fold the garment at the center front, matching the neckpoints, shoulder points, and side seams at the underarm and hem. Insert pins through both layers at the corners marked in Step 5. Mark the pocket location on the remaining garment front with pins or chalk.

Marking the Pocket Placement

Drill Holes

This industry technique is fast and easy, but it frequently leaves permanent holes which will show if the pocket placement is changed or the pocket removed. Using an awl or large sewing machine needle, mark the upper corners 1/4" in from the pocket opening and stitching line.

Tracing Wheel and Dressmaker's Carbon

Frequently used when precision is a must, this method can be used on many fabrics.

Lay out the fabric right sides together or in a single layer right side up for cutting. With the pattern on top, slide the dressmaker's carbon under the fabric. Trace the lines for pocket placement with the tracing wheel. When marking two layers, remove the pattern and turn the layers over. Slide the dressmaker's carbon under the fabric and trace the marked lines.

Tailor Tacks

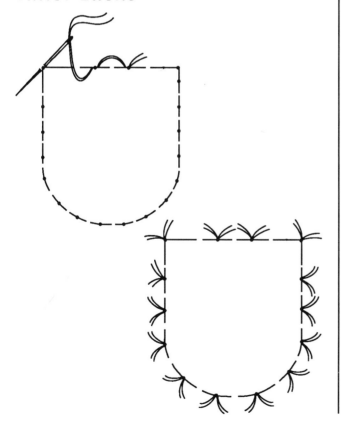

Only used in couture workrooms, this method is very accurate but time-consuming.

When marking two layers, begin with the right sides together and the pocket pattern on top. Using two strands of basting cotton, outline the finished pocket with an uneven basting stitch. At the corners, be sure the needle enters the fabric precisely. Take a stitch beyond the corner before stitching the adjacent side.

Clip the threads on top of the pattern. Then carefully separate the two layers and clip the threads between them.

Thread Tracing

Frequently used with tailor tacks or tracing wheel, thread tracing can be used to mark the most delicate fabrics.

First mark the placement with a tracing wheel or tailor tacks. Right side up, one layer at a time, outline the pocket or pocket opening with a basting stitch. Shorten the stitch for curves and lengthen it for straight lines. Mark corners and ends carefully with a cross.

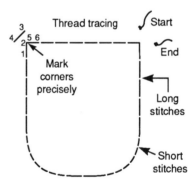

Pins or Disappearing Marking Pens

These shortcut methods are suitable for many everyday fabrics.

Right side up, mark the ends of the pocket opening with very fine pins or a disappearing marking pen.

Interfacings

Depending on the fabric, pocket shape, placement, and use, pockets frequently need an interfacing so they will maintain their shape and to prevent the opening from stretching out of shape. They can be completely interfaced, interfaced only in the hem allowance, or reinforced at the foldline. Suitable interfacing materials include traditional interfacing fabrics, woven tapes, selvages, or seam tape. Generally, a lining is not a substitute for interfacing, but an underlining may be.

Pockets made from crisp, firmly woven fabrics or transparent fabrics are least likely to need interfacings. Pockets made from knits, wools, soft, or flimsy materials are most likely to need them.

The interfacing for the pocket doesn't have to be the same as the interfacings in other parts of the garment. It can have a different application, hand, or weight.

Here are some examples:

A hand-tailored wool jacket: the lapels have hair canvas; the collar, linen; and the pockets, a fusible weft-insertion.

A wool challis skirt: the waistband has a non-woven fusible; the pockets, a fusible knit.

A lightweight silk blouse: the cuffs have self-fabric; the pocket, silk organza.

How to Interface Pockets

Fusible Interfacings

Fusible interfacings are quick and easy to apply. They can be cut to interface the finished pocket area, the finished pocket and hem allowance, the entire pocket including the seam and hem allowances, or just the hem area.

Pockets with fusible interfacings frequently have a smoother, sharper appearance than pockets with no interfacing. They are popular with home-sewers, are found on ready-to-wear

in all price ranges, and are occasionally found on expensive haute couture designs.

Interfaced Pockets

Design Analysis:

Fusible interfacings are suitable for unlined as well as lined pockets. The interfacing for pockets of medium- to heavy-weight fabrics is the same size as the finished pocket; on lightweight fabrics, it extends into the seam and hem allowances.

Suitable interfacing materials include fusible weft-insertions, fusible knit, and fusible woven interfacings. You can make a fusible interfacing by fusing a layer of fusible webbing to a woven sew-in interfacing, silk organza, or other lightweight plain-weave fabrics.

Some favorite fusibles for pockets: Armo Weft, Easy Knit, Fusi-Knit, Knit Fuze, Shape Maker (woven), So Sheer, SofBrush, Stacy Shape-Flex, Suitmaker, Touch O'Gold, Whisper Weft.

Sewing Notes:

1. Select the interfacing. If you have extra fabric scraps, make several samples, using different interfacing materials.

2. Cut the pocket from the fashion fabric. Cut the interfacing section, duplicating the size and shape of the finished pocket.

For a firmer pocket opening, allow the interfacing to extend into the hem allowance 1/2" to 1".

Hints: For many interfacings, you can use this timesaver developed by Milwaukee teacher Margaret Komives. Lay the interfacing over the pocket pattern. You will be able to see through it. Then, using a soft, well-sharpened pencil, trace the stitching lines. When you cut out the interfacing, trim just inside the pencil lines so they won't show through on the fashion fabric.

If the interfacing is opaque, use wax paper to make the interfacing pattern. Or cut the interfacing using the pocket pattern. Then, using the guide on your sewing machine, stitch around the interfacing on the pocket stitching lines and hem foldline to mark the finished size. Trim away the stitched line, seam, and hem allowances.

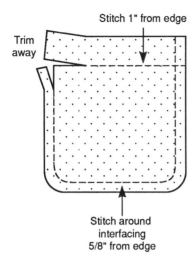

Stitch 1" from edge

Trim away

Stitch around interfacing 5/8" from edge

3. Place the interfacing on the wrong side of the pocket, fusible side down, and fuse it in place, using the manufacturer's directions.

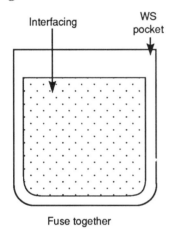

Interfacing

WS pocket

Fuse together

4. Complete the pocket—lined or unlined—and apply it to the garment.

Sew-In Interfacings

Pockets with traditional sew-in interfacings are rarely used today; however, there are occasions when they are the perfect choice. Some favorite sew-ins for pockets: Armo Press, Form Flex Woven, hair canvas, muslin, organza, Sew-in Durapress, Sewin' Sheer, Veri-Shape, Woven Sew-in (Pellon).

Quick-and-Easy Application

Design Analysis:

The interfacing extends into the seam and hem allowances. Since it is stitched into the seamline, a heavy interfacing material is unsuitable.

Generally, this interfacing application is used on lined pockets, although it can be used on unlined ones.

Sewing Notes:

1. Use the pocket pattern to cut one pocket and one interfacing.

2. Wrong sides together, stitch the two layers together just inside the seamline.

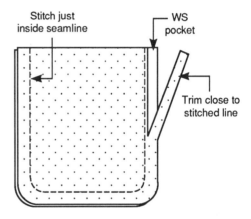

Stitch just inside seamline

WS pocket

Trim close to stitched line

3. Trim the interfacing close to the stitched line.

4. Complete the pocket; and set it to the garment.

Designer Application

Design Analysis:

This couture method is used for lined pockets on fine wool and silk garments and pockets made of heavy or bulky fabrics. Suitable interfacing materials include good-quality woven interfacings, hair canvas, linen, muslin, or silk shantung.

Sewing Notes:

1. Cut one pocket from the fashion fabric. Cut one interfacing section the size of the finished pocket. Then trim all edges 1/8".

2. Using thread tracing, tailor tacks, or chalk, mark the foldline and stitching lines of the pocket.

3. Position the interfacing on the wrong side of the pocket so the top of the interfacing is just below the opening foldline and inside the stitching lines. Using a diagonal basting, baste the centers of the pocket and interfacing together.

4. Use a catchstitch to sew all edges of the interfacing to the pocket.

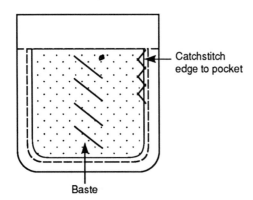

Catchstitch edge to pocket

Baste

5. Wrong side up, press the seam and hem allowances to the wrong side. Catchstitch the raw edges to the interfacing.

> ⌂ *Hints: To control the fullness on curves, use short basting stitches 1/4" from the edge. Miter corners as needed to reduce the bulk.*

6. Wrong side up, press again. Spank the edges with a clapper to flatten them.

> ⌂ *Hint: For really crisp edges, place the pocket on a clean cutting board. Then spank the edges. I cover the floor with a sheet and work on it because my ironing board is too springy.*

7. Complete the pocket with a hand-stitched lining (see page 24) and set the pocket to the garment.

Trenched Application

Design Analysis:

Suitable for lined pockets made from heavy or bulky fabrics, the trenched application is frequently used on tailored jackets.

This application is a favorite of Seattle teacher Jane Whiteley. It features a strip of muslin which forms a trench around the hair canvas interfacing. On the finished pocket, the pocket seam allowances fill the trench without overlapping the hair canvas. The hair canvas and muslin interfacings are cut by the pocket pattern.

Sewing Notes:

1. Using the pocket pattern, cut one pocket from fashion fabric, one interfacing from hair canvas, and one interfacing from muslin.

2. Stitch the two interfacings together 1" from the side and bottom edges and 1/8" below the opening foldline.

3. Trim away the outer edges of the hair canvas close to the stitched line. Trim away the *center* of the muslin close to the stitched line.

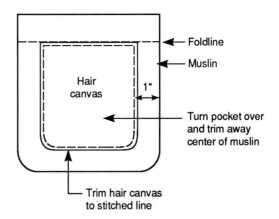

Foldline

Muslin

Hair canvas

1"

Turn pocket over and trim away center of muslin

Trim hair canvas to stitched line

4. Wrong sides up, place the interfacing on the pocket so the hair canvas is next to the fabric pocket and the foldlines match. Pin or hand baste the two layers together.

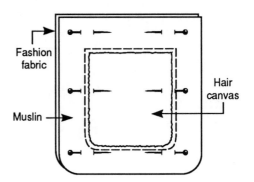

Fashion fabric

Hair canvas

Muslin

5. Wrong sides together, fold the pocket lengthwise and pin the interfacing and pocket together at the raw edges. The raw edges of the muslin will extend slightly beyond the pocket. Baste 1/2" from the edges.

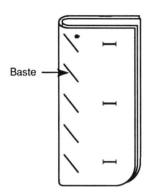

6. Wrong side up, use a loose running stitch to join the two layers at the foldline.

7. Complete the lined pocket by machine and set it to the garment (see page 102).

How to Interface Hems

Suitable for frequently used pockets made from firmly woven fabrics, the interfaced pocket hem is quicker and easier to make than the interfaced pocket. The interfacing is cut with the least amount of stretch (usually the lengthwise grain) parallel to the opening so that it reinforces the pocket opening and prevents the opening from stretching out of shape. Interfaced hems are suitable for lined and unlined pockets, and both fusible and sew-in interfacings can be used.

Design Analysis:

Fusible interfacings interface the finished hem area. They should not extend into the seam allowances at the sides of the opening or onto the pocket itself.

Sew-in interfacings can interface the entire hem or just the finished hem area.

Sewing Notes:

Wrong side up, fuse or baste the interfacing to the hem allowance. Then complete the pocket.

On unlined pockets made from lightweight fabrics, you may prefer to use the interfacing to finish the hem edge too. Right sides together, join the interfacing and hem edge with a 1/4" seam. Understitch and press the interfacing to the wrong side. Fold the pocket at the foldline—the raw edge of the interfacing should touch the foldline. If it is too wide, trim as needed. Then complete the pocket.

 Hint: This is the same as the face-the-facing technique you've probably used many times.

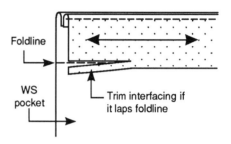

Reinforced Openings

Many pockets don't need to be interfaced; however, if the opening isn't reinforced, the pocket will stretch out of shape during construction, pressing, or use.

Design Analysis:

The reinforced opening has a narrow (1/4" to 1/2" wide) stabilizer centered over the foldline or just inside on the hem allowance. Materials such as purchased hem tapes or plain weave tapes, selvages from lightweight blouse fabrics, and strips of fusible interfacing make good stabilizers.

Sewing Notes:

1. Preshrink the stabilizer before applying it.

2. When using a strip of fusible interfacing, cut the strip on the lengthwise grain. Wrong side of the pocket up, place the interfacing on the hem allowance with one edge touching the foldline. Fuse the strip in place.

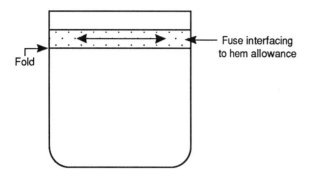

Fold

Fuse interfacing
to hem allowance

When using tapes or selvage, center the tape over the foldline, and machine or hand stitch the tape just inside the opening.

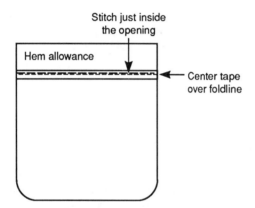

Stitch just inside
the opening

Hem allowance

Center tape
over foldline

Underlining Pockets

Generally, when the garment is underlined for color or opaqueness, the pocket will also be underlined to preserve the integrity of the design.

Design Analysis:

The underlining is cut the same size as the pocket. Depending on the fabrics used, pocket shape, and desired effect, the underlining may replace the interfacing or it may be used with an interfacing.

Sewing Notes:

1. Using the pocket pattern, cut one pocket from the fashion fabric and one from the underlining. Generally, both are cut on the lengthwise grain; however, when the pocket is cut on a different grain, the underlining is usually cut on the lengthwise grain unless it will affect the appearance of the pocket.

2. On the pocket, clip-mark each end of the foldline. On the underlining, mark the foldline with chalk or tracing wheel and dressmaker's carbon.

3. Interface the pocket as needed by applying the interfacing to the underlining. (See Interfacings on page 94.)

4. Wrong sides up, place the underlining on top of the pocket, matching the foldlines. Baste the layers together at the center.

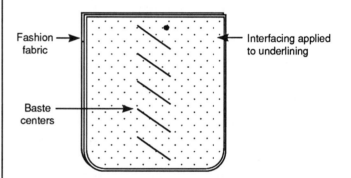

Fashion
fabric

Interfacing applied
to underlining

Baste
centers

Baste the pocket and underlining together 1/2" from the edges.

Hint: For a smoother pocket, curl the raw edges toward the wrong side so the edges of the underlining extend beyond those of the pocket; then baste.

5. Wrong side up, join the two layers at the foldline.

Hints: On better garments, I use a loose running stitch and pick up just the back of the fashion fabric so the stitches will be invisible on the right side of the pocket.

On everyday designs, machine stitch on the foldline.

6. For an unlined pocket, finish the raw edge of the pocket hem. Then, right sides together, fold the pocket at the foldline, and stitch the seams at each side.

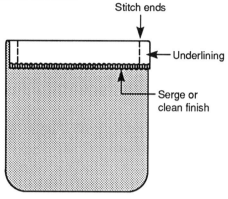

Turn the pocket right side out; press. Then, using your favorite method, complete the unlined pocket and set it to the garment.

7. For a lined pocket, join the pocket and lining. Then, using your favorite method, complete the lined pocket and set it to the garment.

Finishes for Pocket Openings

Patch pocket openings can be finished many different ways, depending on the shape of the opening, garment style, pocket design, and pocket application.

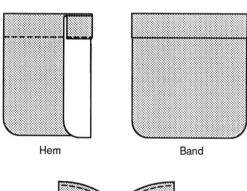

Hem   Band

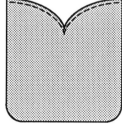

Shaped edge

If the edge is straight, it can be finished with a hem, band, facing (see page 13), edge-to-edge lining (see page 27), or binding (see page 102); but if it is shaped, it can't be finished with a hem.

This section focuses on hems and hem finishes *for straight edges* and facings *for shaped edges*. When sewing other pocket designs, check the index for the appropriate section.

Traditional Hems

Design Analysis:

The traditional 1"- to 1-1/2"-wide hem is one of the least conspicuous finishes. The hem allowance is a mirror image of the pocket top. On lined pockets the edge is left unfinished since the lining will cover it. This hem is well-suited for tailored garments and quality fabrics, while the narrow topstitched hem may be more attractive on sportswear and casual designs.

On unlined pockets, the raw edge of the hem is finished as flatly as possible. There are a variety of different ways to do this, depending on the fabric, available time and equipment, and garment quality.

Pattern Development:

1. On the finished pocket pattern, draw the edge of the hem parallel to the pocket opening and 1" to 1-1/2" below the opening.

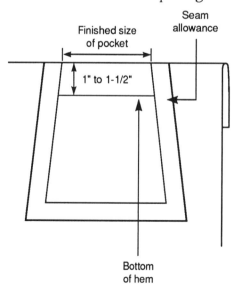

2. Fold the tracing paper. Align with the opening and trace the sides and bottom of the hem.

3. Add seam allowances if you haven't already.

4. With the new pocket pattern in the folded position, cut away the excess paper at the sides. Open the pattern flat, and trim away any excess at the top and bottom.

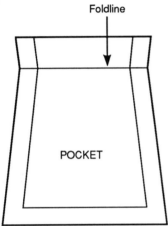

Foldline

POCKET

Sewing Notes for Finishing Hems: Clean Finished

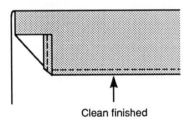

Clean finished

In the fashion industry, "clean finish" describes the finish homesewers call turned-and-stitched. To further muddy the waters, the pattern companies consider any edge finish that prevents raveling a clean finish. The name isn't really important except when you're trying to communicate.

This finish is suitable for lightweight fabrics, but even then it may create a ridge which shows on the outside of the pocket.

Add 1/4" to the hem allowance when making the pattern. Fold the edge under 1/4" and edgestitch. For neat, even stitching, use the inside of your regular presser foot as an edgestitching guide.

Folded Edge

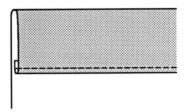

Folded edge

Used on shirts and other lightweight fabrics, the folded edge is frequently stitched to the wrong side of the pocket.

Press the hem allowance to the wrong side of the pocket. Press the raw edge of the hem under 1/4". Then edgestitch it in place.

Hints: To be sure the line is straight on the right side of the pocket, use a piece of drafting tape on the machine bed as a stitching gauge. Right side up, align the top of the pocket with the gauge and stitch.

When using this finish on transparent fabric, trim after you've pressed the folded edge under so the edge is even and has no zigs and zags. Edgestitch. Then stitch again 1/4" away to make the folded edge a part of the design. Now the hem has an opaque stripe created by the three layers of fabric.

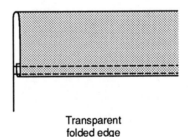

Transparent folded edge

Here is another idea for transparent fabrics. Make the hem allowance twice the finished hem depth. Wrong side up, press first on the foldline. Then fold the hem allowance so that the raw edge touches the foldline. Press again. If desired, stitch the hem in place.

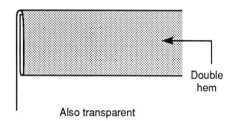

Double hem

Also transparent

Pinked

The pinked edge is suitable for light- to medium-weight fabrics which are opaque and don't ravel badly. Pinking is a viable alternative to zigzagging or serging.

Stitch 1/4" from the raw edge. Then pink the edge.

Raw Edge

Suitable for lined pockets, non-woven fabrics, and knits which don't roll or stretch. The raw edge isn't appropriate for fabrics which ravel.

This finish looks a little better if you stitch 1/4" from the edge.

Seam Tape

Frequently used on medium-weight and bulky fabrics, seam tape covers the raw edge. It also stabilizes the opening so the pocket won't stretch out of shape.

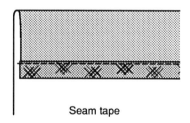

Seam tape

Right sides up, place the seam tape on the pocket hem so that it overlaps the edge about 1/4". Edgestitch the tape in place.

 Hint: *Always shrink the seam tape before sewing.*

Serged

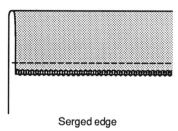

Serged edge

Fast and easy, this is the best finish for most fabrics and most garments. It isn't suitable for your finest couture designs, but you'll probably line those pockets anyway. If you have a choice, use a two- or three-thread serger and fine thread so less thread is laid down.

If you don't have a serger, this is a good time to ask your local sewing machine dealer for a demonstration.

Turned-and-Stitched

See Clean Finished on page 100.

Zigzagged or Multi-stitch Zigzagged

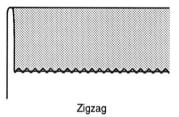

Zigzag

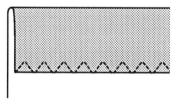

Multi-stitch zigzag

These finishes are suitable for medium-weight and bulky fabrics, but on lightweight fabrics, they may cause the edge to tunnel or roll. I think the multi-stitch zigzag or serpentine stitch rolls less than the regular zigzag, but it takes longer and not all machines can make this stitch. To zigzag, set the machine for W,2-L,2; for a multi-stitch zigzag, set it W,4-L,1. Right side up, stitch 3/8" from the edge. Then trim the hem allowance close to the stitched line.

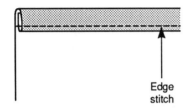
Narrow Topstitched Hems

Edge
stitch

Narrow hems are frequently used on casual designs and jeans. The finished hem width and fabric weight will determine the amount of fabric needed for the hem allowance, but it is generally 5/8" to 1" wide.

Press the hem to the wrong side. Then fold the raw edge under and press again. Edgestitch the hem in place.

Bindings

Unlike facings, which turn completely to the inside or outside, bindings are as wide as the seam allowance and cover both sides of the opening. You can bind the upper edge of a pocket with any fabric—it doesn't have to be bias binding if the edge is straight. If you plan to use purchased binding, ribbon, ribbing, or braid, you won't need a pattern for the binding. Measure the pocket to determine the length needed, including seam allowances at each end.

To determine the width needed to cover both the front and back of the opening seam allowance, multiply the finished width of the binding by 5. This allows a turn-under on the underside of the opening.

To apply, pin the binding to the pocket opening, right sides together. Fold the ends of the binding in and press. Stitch, wrap the binding over the opening, and baste. Ditch-stitch by hand or machine.

See page 33 for more detailed instructions.

Setting the Pocket

Pockets—lined and unlined—can be applied by hand or machine. Generally, pockets made of light- to medium-weight fabrics are topstitched to the garment, while pockets made of heavier fabrics are applied by hand to avoid distorting the pocket and/or garment. In ready-to-wear, pockets are usually machine-stitched; in couture, they are generally hand-stitched.

Decide how the pocket will be applied before making the pocket pattern. If it will be applied by topstitching more than 1/4" from the edges, the underside of the pocket will show and the pocket will need wider seam allowances, mitered corners, faced edges, or an attractive lining.

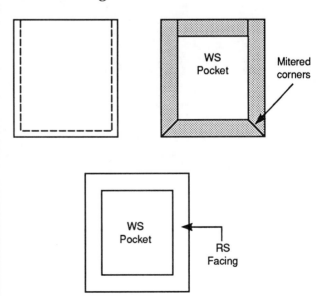

WS Pocket

Mitered corners

WS Pocket

WS Pocket

RS Facing

General Directions for Applying Patch Pockets

1. Complete the pocket. (See Unlined and Lined Pockets on pages 2 and 21.)

2. Press the pockets. (See Pressing Techniques on page 105.)

3. Mark the pocket location on the garment. (See Marking the Pocket Placement on page 93).

4. Reinforce the pocket area on the garment section as needed. (See Reinforcing the Garment on page 106.)

5. Right sides up, pin the pocket to the garment. If the garment section is flat, work with the section flat on the table. If it is shaped, place the section over a pressing cushion or ham; then pin the pocket in place.

 Hint: The pocket should have enough ease so it won't pull when you insert your hand, but it shouldn't have so much that it gaps. Clotilde places a crumpled tissue between the pocket and garment section; then she pins the pocket in place.

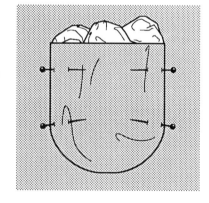

Put crumpled tissue in pocket before pinning to garment section

6. Baste as needed.

 Hint: Basting aids such as water-soluble glue sticks and fusible webs are easy to use and enable you to stitch perfectly the first time.

When using a fusible web, I prefer Wonder-Under, which has a paper release sheet. I cut it into 1/4" wide strips; and apply it to the pocket seam allowances before pinning the pocket in place. Then I fuse the pocket in place with a little steam.

For better garments, I always hand baste. First baste through the pocket center using a diagonal stitch. Then baste the sides and bottom about 1/4" from the edge.

7. Stitch the pocket in place. (See Machine-stitched Applications and Hand-stitched Applications below.) Reinforce the corners appropriately for the pocket's use and garment's design. (See Reinforcing the Corners on page 105.)

8. Press, using either a Teflon plate on your iron or a press cloth to protect your fabric.

Machine-stitched Applications

Before the pocket pattern is made, decide how the pocket will be sewn to the garment—by topstitching or edgestitching by hand or machine, or by invisible hand-stitching.

If the pocket will be sewn close to the edges, it can be made with regular 5/8" seam allowances. If it will be sewn more than 1/4" from the edge, it may require an edge-to-edge lining, a hand-applied lining, wider seam allowances, or a facing.

The size of the seam allowance also affects topstitching. If the topstitching is far enough from the edge that the presser foot will be half on, half off the seam allowance, your topstitching may wobble. In that case, use a zipper foot.

Also use a zipper foot or straight-stitch foot for better visibility or use a blind-hem or edgestitch foot.

Adjust the stitch length. Lengthen it for sportswear and shorten it for dressy designs.

 Hint: A short stitch length is easier to control.

For a dressier finish, edgestitch 1/16" from the pocket edge.

For a sporty look, topstitch 1/4" from the edge, and, if desired, stitch again at the edge.

To make frequently used pockets sturdy, topstitch twice or stitch using a twin or triple needle.

To highlight the stitching, use buttonhole twist, machine embroidery thread (size 30), or two strands of regular thread.

Begin stitching at the upper right corner as you look at the pocket. Continue around the pocket to the upper left corner. See page 105 for ways to reinforce pocket corners.

Ordinarily, you would begin and end with backstitches. But when sewing better garments, leave long threads at the beginning and end. When finished, pull the threads to the underside and knot them in an overhand knot. For security, you can dot the knot with Fray Check.

When stitching naps, stitch each side from the corner to the bottom center. Cut the threads. Pull them to the wrong side and knot.

Topstitched Pockets

On this pocket, the topstitching doesn't always follow the edge of the pocket, so the pocket must be lined attractively with an edge-to-edge lining (see page 27). The topstitching can be stitched on the pocket before the pocket is attached or the topstitching can be used to attach the pocket to the garment.

Hint: *Pat Whittemore, who tested the instructions for this book, cuts a topstitching template from freezer paper. She then irons the template, shiny side down, to the pocket and stitches around it.*

Sewing Notes—Method One

These directions are for a pocket which is topstitched, then applied to the garment, so you'll make a topstitching template.

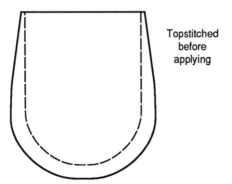

Topstitched before applying

1. On tracing or freezer paper, trace the finished pocket, draw the topstitching design on it, and cut out the paper template.

Hint: *If the pocket is symmetrical, draw the design for half the pocket. Fold the pattern at the center and cut on the topstitching.*

2. Baste the topstitching template to the pocket. On firm fabrics, baste with pins or tape. On flimsy materials, draw around the template. If you used freezer paper, press the shiny side to the front of the pocket.

3. Stitch next to the edge of the topstitching template. To stitch accurately, use a zipper, edge stitch, blind hem, straight-stitch, or Bernina jeans foot.

4. Right sides up, pin the pocket to the garment. Baste through all layers next to the topstitching.

5. From the wrong side of the garment, secure the pocket with a short running stitch using the basting line as a guide.

Sewing Notes—Method Two

These directions are for a pocket which is topstitched and set simultaneously.

1. Make a topstitching template using the directions above and baste it to the pocket.

2. Right sides up, pin the pocket to the garment.

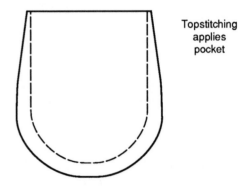

Topstitching applies pocket

3. To set the pocket, topstitch around the template.

Hand-stitched Applications

Set the pocket by hand on heavy, expensive, and special-occasion fabrics. Since this application is used only on very expensive ready-to-wear and couture garments, use it with discretion to avoid a "loving hands at home" look.

First baste the pocket in place. With the garment wrong side up, use the basting as a stitching guide. Use a running stitch for decorative pockets or a short diagonal stitch for functional pockets. For greater security, hand sew twice or use a catchstitch.

Hints: *Locate the stitches 1/16" to 1/8" from the pocket edge so the pocket doesn't look tight or doesn't pucker at the edges.*

Make the stitches carefully so that they catch only the seam and hem allowances (or lining) and do not show on the pocket itself.

Secure the upper corners well so no raw edges peek out and so the pocket won't rip off when used.

When a hand-set pocket has topstitching, topstitch the pocket before sewing it to the garment. In fact, on most pockets it's better to topstitch before lining the pocket.

Reinforced Pocket Corners

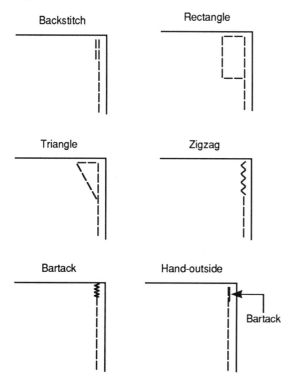

Backstitch

Rectangle

Triangle

Zigzag

Bartack

Hand-outside

Bartack

On frequently used pockets, reinforce the upper corners by machine with a backstitch, rectangle, triangle, zigzag, or bartack. Spottacks—stitching in place—may not be strong enough for pockets which will be used.

Or reinforce the corners by hand with a bar tack on the outside of the garment or catchstitches on the inside.

WS Garment

Pressing Techniques

Unlined Pockets

1. Machine stitch around the pocket just inside the seamline.

2. Wrong side up, fold the seam and hem allowances to the wrong side, rolling the stitched line so you can barely see it at the folded edges.

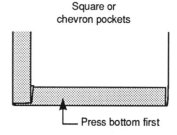

Square or chevron pockets

Press bottom first

On square or chevron pockets, press the bottom edge first; then press the sides.

On curved pockets, machine stitch again midway between the seamline and raw edge. Pull up the bobbin thread and adjust the gathers in the curved sections so the seam allowances fit smoothly on the wrong side of the pocket.

Hints: *For perfect pockets, use a cardboard template the size and shape of the finished pocket. Insert it between the pocket and seam allowances to press accurately.*

Some of my students like the Pocket Former—a gadget that holds the fabric in place for you while you're pressing curved edges (see Supply List on page 113). Don't forget that each corner on this little gadget has a different curve, so use the same curve to press both corners of the pocket.

3. Trim and notch the seam allowances around the curves so they lie flat.

Lined Pockets

For a smoother seamline, press the pocket/lining seam allowances in separate directions to allow the pocket seam allowance to lie flat. Here's how:

1. Right sides together, join the lining and pocket at the hem allowance. Press toward lining. Understitch. Fold pocket hem allowance, right sides together.

2. Right sides together, join the sides and bottom of the pocket and lining. Press the seamlines flat.

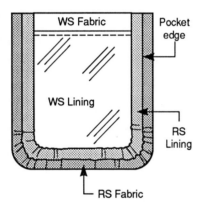

3. With the lining side up, press the lining seam allowances toward the lining.

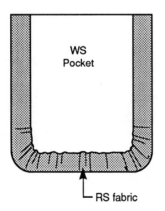

4. Turn the pocket over. Press the pocket seam allowances toward the pocket.

Trim and notch the seam allowances around the curves so they lie flat. Then turn the pocket right side out. Slash the pocket as needed if you haven't left an opening for turning.

5. Lining side up, adjust the lining so you can see the seamline at the edge. Press lightly with steam.

6. Turn the pocket right side up and, if necessary, shape it. (See Shaping the Pocket below.)

Shaping the Pocket

If the pocket will be applied to a close-fitting design, shape it to fit the garment and body curves which it will cover.

Right side up, place the pocket over the ham. Cover the pocket with a press cloth. Press lightly with a steam iron. Let the pocket cool before moving it so it will retain its shape.

Reinforcing the Garment Under the Pocket

If the garment section is underlined, the pocket area may not need additional reinforcement.

If the pocket will receive a lot of use and abuse, reinforce the entire garment underneath the pocket by applying the interfacing to the wrong side of the garment.

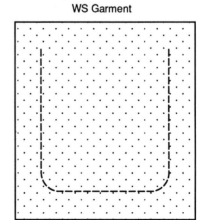

Reinforce entire area

For most garments, I prefer to reinforce with woven sew-in interfacings because they won't change the color, texture, or hand of the fashion fabric. Preshrunk muslin and hair canvas are two of my favorites.

You can also use fusible interfacings. Trim the edges with pinking shears to avoid a ridge. Always test on fabric scraps before applying fusibles to the garment section to check for a demarcation line. Also check to be sure the fusible doesn't make the garment fabric too stiff in the pocket area.

If it will receive little or no use, use 1" squares of interfacing at the upper corners.

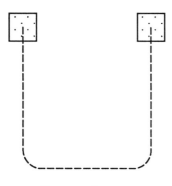

1" square at corners

If the use will be somewhere in between, reinforce the area under the upper third of the pocket.

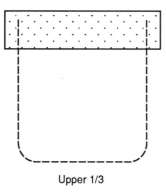

Upper 1/3

Hints for Special Fabrics

While many fabrics are special and deserve their own hints, we can't cover *everything* in this book. Here are hints on two fabrics:

Plaids

On plaid designs, the pattern on the pocket should match the garment on both sides and at the bottom. On some garments, particularly men's and ladies' tailored jackets which have darts under the pocket, the plaid on the pocket will not match the plaid on the garment at the pocket opening.

On casual designs, the pocket is sometimes cut on the bias. Before cutting pockets on the bias, examine current trends to see if it is fashionable.

To match the plaid on the garment and pocket:

1. Make a pocket pattern without hem and seam allowances.

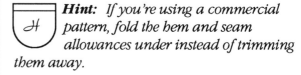 ***Hint:*** *If you're using a commercial pattern, fold the hem and seam allowances under instead of trimming them away.*

2. On the right side of the garment section, mark the pocket placement with thread tracing, tailor tacks, chalk, or a disappearing marking pen.

3. Right side up, spread the garment section on the table. Place the pocket pattern on the garment section, aligning it with the placement lines. On the sides and bottom of the pocket pattern, trace and label the fabric's color bars.

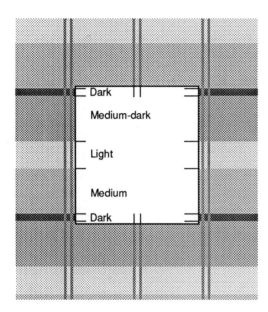

Place pattern on garment
section and mark color bars

Hint: *For a perfect garment, repeat for each pocket. Sometimes there are slight differences between the right and left sides.*

4. Add hem and seam allowances to the pocket pattern.

5. Right sides up, lay the pocket pattern on the fabric so that the color bars are aligned. Cut out the pocket.

Sweater Knits

Sweater knit pockets tend to stretch when topstitched. Use this clever technique instead.

1. It's easiest to use a finished edge for the top of the pocket, such as ribbing from a sweater body. Cut 5/8" side and bottom seam allowances.

2. Press the side seam allowances to the inside.

3. Mark the bottom and side edges of the pocket on the finished garment with thread tracing.

4. Lay the pocket on the garment at the bottom seam allowance, right sides together. The pocket will be upside-down.

5. Stitch across the bottom of the pocket and the turned-in side seams with a 5/8" seam allowance. Backstitch at each end.

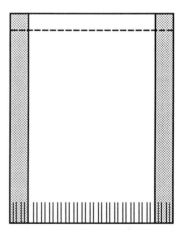

6. Fold the pocket up into place, pin, and handstitch the side seam allowances from the back.

Designer's Workshop

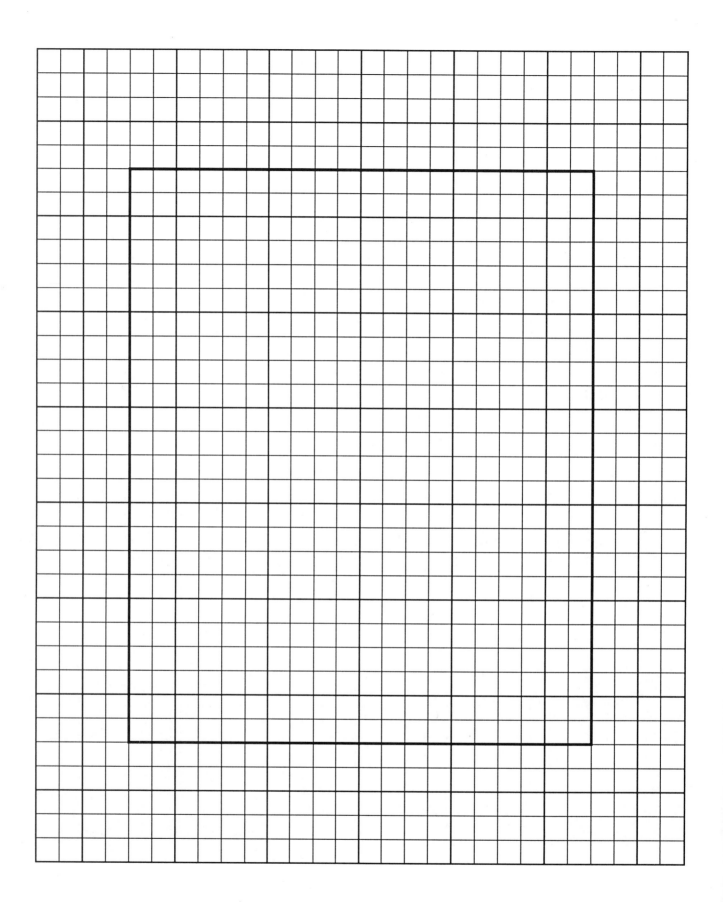

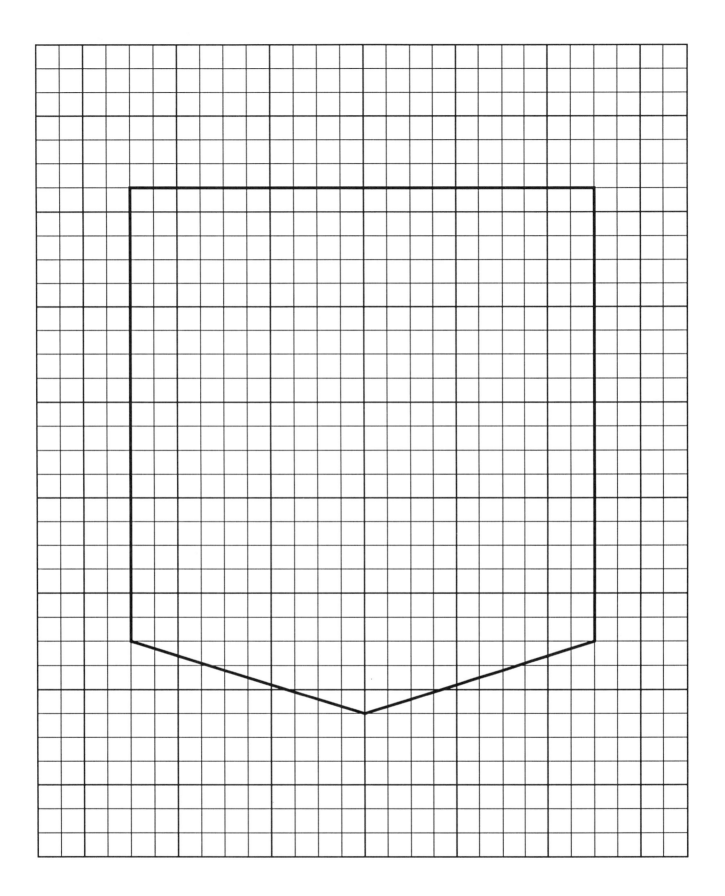

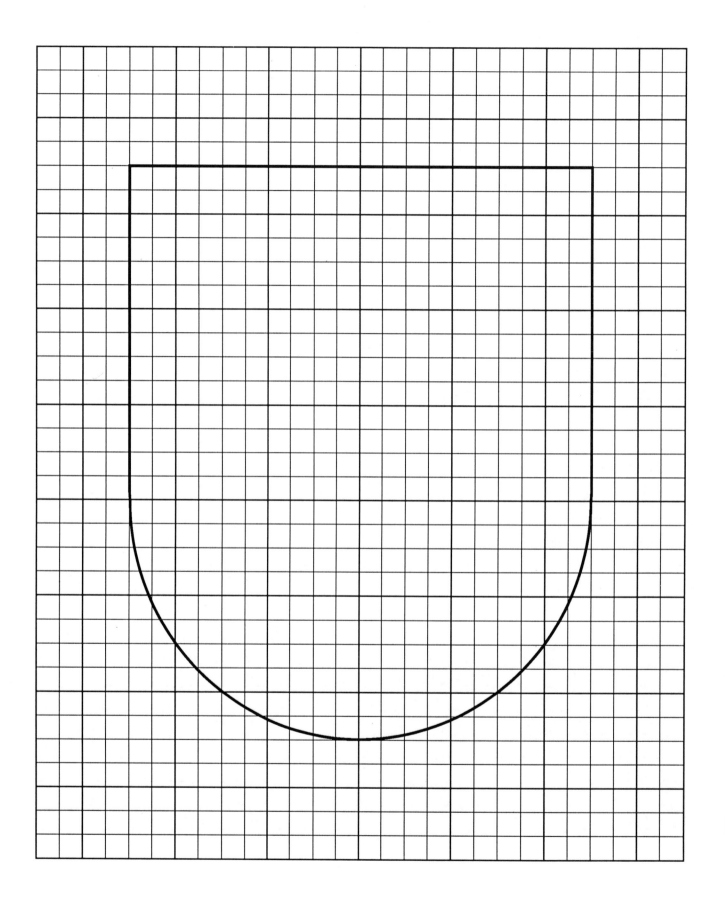

Sources

Aardvark Adventures
PO Box 2449
Livermore, CA 94551
(415)443-2687

Clotilde
2 Sew Smart Way, B8031
Stevens Point, WI 54481-8031
(305) 761-8655

Home-Sew
Bethlehem, PA 18018
Nancy's Notions
PO Box 683
Beaver Dam, WI 53916
(414)887-0391

National Thread & Supply
695 Red Oak Rd
Stockbridge, GA 30281
(800)847-1001

Newark Dressmaker Supply
PO Box 2448
Lehigh Valley, PA 18001
(215)837-7500

Sew/Fit Co
PO Box 565
LaGrange, IL 60525
(312)579-3222

Treadleart
25834 Narbonne Ave, Ste I
Lomita, CA 90717
(800)327-4222

Publications

The Creative Machine Newsletter
PO Box 2634
Menlo Park, CA 94026
Quarterly, $12/year

Sew News
PO Box 1790
Peoria, IL 61656
Monthly, $15.97/year

Sewer's SourceLetter
7509 7th Pl SW
Seattle, WA 98106
Quarterly, $15/year

Sewing Update, Serging Update
c/o Sew News above
Bimonthly, $19.50/year;

Threads
63 S. Main St
Newtown, CT 06470
Bimonthly, $22/year

Treadleart
25834 Narbonne Ave, Ste I
Lomita, CA 90717
Bimonthly, $18/year

Glossary

*If you need more help with basic sewing techniques, consult **Claire Shaeffer's Fabric Sewing Guide** (see page 115 for ordering information).*

Appliqué One fabric applied to another.

Backstitch Secure stitching by stitching backwards a few stitches.

Bartack Satin stitch for 1/4" to 1/2".

Baste Sew to hold two layers together temporarily.

Bias strip Fabric cut at 45 angle to lengthwise and crosswise grain.

Binding Fabric used to enclose an edge.

Blind-hem stitch A hemming stitch on the sewing machine.

Blindstitch Small v-shaped hemming stitches hidden between the hem and the garment.

Bodkin A tool to pull elastic or cord through a casing.

Casing Hem or area through which elastic or ties are threaded.

Catchstitch Elongated cross stitches used to hem garments and to secure pocket edges.

Chevron A v-shaped pattern of stripes.

Clapper Wooden tool used in pressing.

Clean finish A method for finishing the raw edges of pocket hems.

Clips Short snips perpendicular to the edge and into the fabric to mark something, such as a pocket opening.

Crimping A technique for easing fabric into the seamline by holding a finger behind the presser foot and impeding the flow of fabric under the foot (also called ease-plus, stay-stitching plus, or crowding).

Cross tuck A tuck that crosses another tuck at an angle.

Disappearing pen Air- or water-soluble marking pen

Ditch stitch Stitching from the top side of the fabric in the well or ditch of the seam.

Double-fold bias A bias strip of fabric where both long raw edges are folded to the center, then the folds matched in a second fold.

Ease baste A temporary stitch used to ease excess fullness into a seamline. Using a regular stitch length, a tight bobbin tension, and a heavier thread on the bobbin, stitch right side up just inside the seamline and again midway between the raw edge and seamline. Pull both threads up together so they won't break.

Edgestitching Topstitching 1/16" from the edge or seamline.

Fabric hand The way the fabric feels and drapes.

Fell stitch Neat tiny vertical stitches used in tailoring

Foldline The fold at the pocket opening.

Fusible web A weblike like adhesive which melts when you apply heat and moisture. Some fusible webs, such as TransFuse and Wonder-Under are applied to paper so they can be ironed onto fabric without a protective sheet.

Glue-baste Using a glue stick instead of thread to hold fabrics together temporarily.

Grade To reduce the bulk of enclosed seams by trimming the individual seam allowances different widths, clipping inward curves and corners, notching convex curves, and trimming away excess fabric at outward corners.

Grain The direction the fibers are woven or knit, either lengthwise or crosswise.

Gusset An extra piece of fabric between the top pocket and the bottom pocket or fabric.

Hem allowance The amount of fabric turned to the inside at the pocket opening.

"Invisible" stitching Stitching on the lining in such a way that the pocket rolls over and hides the stitching.

Matchpoints Drawn lines that intersect a shape and are used to match pocket and garment or lining points exactly.

Miter To join two adjacent edges at an angle, frequently a 45° angle.

Nap Short, fuzzy fibers on fabric surface; one-direction design that must be cut with all pattern pieces laid in the same direction.

Pintuck A narrow channel of fabric stitched together.

Pleat depth The distance between the outside fold of a pleat and the inside fold.

Pocket Former A metal gadget into which you press fabric to get an exact corner shape.

Ravel To fray.

Running stitch Short, permanent hand stitches.

Satin stitch Zigzag stitch of any width with a very short length (.5 or less).

Selvage Finished edges on each side of a woven fabric, running parallel to the lengthwise grain.

Serger A machine that overcasts and trims an edge simultaneously.

Setting the pocket Applying the pocket to the garment.

Slipstitch A hand stitch used to join two layers of fabric from the right side.

Spank the edge Press a clapper against a folded edge to get a sharp crease.

Spottack Make several stitches in one place to secure the thread.

Taper Make gradually smaller toward the end.

Template A shape made of another substance, such as cardboard or freezer paper, usually the size of the finished pocket.

Thread tracing Hand basting used to mark stitching lines and pocket placement.

Toile Test garment made of muslin.

Topstitching Stitching on the right side of the pocket (not necessarily to attach the pocket to the garment)

Tuck strip A strip of paper inserted in the pocket pattern to expand it for tucks.

Understitch Technique of stitching by hand or machine through the facing and seam allowances.

Bibliography

Hutton, Jessie, and Gladys Cunningham. *Singer Sewing Book*. New York: Golden Press, 1972.

Ladbury, Ann. *The Dressmaker's Dictionary*. New York: Arco Publishing, Inc., 1982.

Lawrence, Judy, and Clotilde Yurick. *Sew Smart*. Minneapolis, MN: Burgess Publishing Co., 1978.

Mansfield, Evelyn A. *Clothing Construction*. Boston: Houghton Mifflin Co., 1953.

Picken, Mary Brooks. *Sewing Magic*. New York: McGraw-Hill Book Co., Inc., 1952.

Reader's Digest Complete Guide to Sewing. Pleasantville, NY: The Reader's Digest Association, Inc., 1976.

*Shaeffer, Claire B. *Claire Shaeffer's Sewing S.O.S.* Menlo Park, CA: Open Chain Publishing, 1988.

Claire Shaffer's Fabric Sewing Guide. Radnor, PA: Chilton Book Co., 1989.

The Complete Book of Sewing Short Cuts. New York: Sterling Publishing Co., Inc., 1981.

Tate, Sharon Lee. *Inside Fashion Design*. New York: Harper & Row Publishers, Inc., 1989.

Wolfe, Mary Gorgen. *Clear-Cut Pattern Making*. New York: John Wiley & Sons, 1982.

Zieman, Nancy, and Robbie Fanning. *The Busy Woman's Sewing Book*. Menlo Park, CA: Open Chain Publishing, 1988.

* (All three Claire Shaeffer books available autographed from Box 157, Palm Spring, CA 92263.)

Index

Ahles, Carol, *viii*
All-purpose application for flaps, 88
Anatomy, *v*
Applying patch pockets, 103
Band, Pleated Pocket With, 67
   Pockets with, 10, 12
   Shaped, 70
Band-aid pocket, *viii*
Banded Pocket With Flared Pleat, 68
Basic Lined Pocket, 2, 21
Bellows Pocket With Flap, 78
Bellows Pocket With Separate Gusset, 75
Bellows Pockets, 71
Bias grainline, *x*
Bias-cut flap, 87
Binding on corners, 33
Binding, 19, 102
Blind tuck, 50
Blind-hem stitch, 36
Blindstitch, 89
Bodkin, 18
Bound Edge, Self-Lined Pocket, 32
Box pleats, 59, 60, 64
Bubble, 87
Bulk, reducing, 37
Button formula, 6
Buttonhole location, 37
Cargo pockets, 61
Catchstitch, 96
Chevron corners, pressing, 3
Clean finished hems, 100
Clear-Cut Pattern Making, 92
Closed inverted pleat, 60
Clotilde, 103
Corded tucks, 49
Corners, pressing, 3
   Reinforced, 105
Couture application for flaps, 90
Couture Lined Pocket, 24
Couture method for interfacing, 95
Couture, 105
Crimp, 3
Cross Tucks, Pocket With, 54
Cross tucks, 49, 50
Cuffs, 43
Curved corners, 35
Curved pocket with binding, 33
Curved pockets, corners, pressing, 3
Custom-made shirt, 5
Cut-on cuff, 43, 45
Decorative Edge-to-Edge Lining, 27
Decorative Faced Opening, 15
Design pocket, *viii*
Designer application for interfacing, 95
Designer Method, hem finish, 3
Disappearing marking pens, 93
Dodson, Jackie, 5
Dress shirts, English-made, 6
Dressmaker Method, hem finish, 3
Dressmaker's carbon, 93

Ease baste, 3
Easy Lined Patch, 23, 82
Easy Tucked Pocket, 51
Edges, Faced, 13
Elastic, braided, 18
Elasticized Opening, 17
Envelope, using to find bias, *x*
Everything, 1+
Expanding pocket, 71
Fabrics, special, 107
Face-the-facing, 15, 97
Faced Edges, 13
Faced Opening, Decorative, 15
Facing, Ribbon, 14
Fake Inside-Stitched Pocket, 34
Fell stitch, 89
Finishes, 99
Flap application for lightweight fabrics, 90
Flap Applications, 88
Flap, Bellows Pocket With, 78
Flap, Pleated Pocket With, 70
Flap, Saddle Bag With, 79
Flaps, 85+
Flared Pleat, Banded Pocket With, 68
Flat-Lined Pocket, 26
Flat-lined bellows, 71
Folded edge hems, 100
Freezer paper, 4, 104
Fusible interfacings, 94, 107
Fusible web, 103
Garment, reinforcing under, 106
Gathered Pocket With Band, 12
Gathered Pouch, 19
General Directions for Patch Pockets, 91
Giuntini, Miss, 39
Grainline, bias, *x*
Gussets, 75
Hair canvas, 96
Hand-stitched applications, 105
Hathaway shirt, 5
Hem finishes, 3
Hem, Tucked, 8
Hems, interfaced, 97
   Traditional, 99
Hints, *viii*
Hook Method, 29
How to Use This Book, *vi*
Inside-Stitched Pocket, 39
Interfacings, 94
Inverted pleats, 59, 60
Invisible stitching, 89
Jeans Pocket, 7
Kangaroo Pocket, 4
Knife pleats, 59, 61
Komives, Margaret, 94
Land's End shirt, 5
Lined bellows, 71
Lined Patch Pockets, 20+
Lined Pocket With Cut-on Cuff, 43
Linings, 20

Location, 92
Machine-stitched applications, 103
Magic-Lined Patch Pocket, 35
Man's Shirt Pocket, 5
Mann, Liz, 40
Marking placement, 93
Military pocket, 71
Miter, double, 73
Mr. Michael, *viii*
Multi-stitch zigzagged hems, 101
Muslin, 96
Narrow topstitched hems, 102
Nix-Rice, Nancy, 1, 3
Notched Tucks, Pocket With, 57
Notched tucks, 49
Novelty Pockets, 38+
One-Piece cuff, 47
One-Piece Self-Lined Pockets, 30
One-piece flap, 87
Open inverted pleat, 60
Opening, Elasticized, 17
Overlapping tucks, 53
Paper for patterns, *x*
Paper, freezer, 4
Patches, Pocket, 82, 84
Pattern development for flaps, 86
Pattern paper, *x*
Patterns, general directions for making, *x*
Pencil slot, 6
Pinked hems, 101
Pinking shears, 37
Pintucks, 49, 50
Placement, 92
Plaids, 107
Pleat depth, 60
Pleat Terminology, 60
Pleat underlay, 61
Pleated Pocket With Band, 67
Pleated Pocket With Flap, 70
Pleated Pocket With Shaped Band, 70
Pleated Pockets, 59
Pleats, 59
Pocket Former, 4, 106
Pocket location, 6, 21, 92
Pocket Patch With Bound Edges, 84
Pocket Patches, 82
Pocket placement, 92
Pocket With Box Pleat, 64
Pocket With Cross Tucks, 54
Pocket With Inverted Pleat, 61, 63
Pocket With Notched Tucks, 57
Pocket With Overlapping Tucks, 53
Pocket With Pintucks, 50
Pockets With Tucks, 49
Pouch, Gathered, 19
Pressing seams, 22
Pressing techniques, 105
Pressing, 3
Quick-and-easy application for interfacing, 95
Rabbit ears, 88
Ralph Lauren shirt, 5
Raw edge hems, 101
Reinforced openings, 97
Reinforced pocket corners, 105

Reinforcing under the garment, 106
Reverse Tucks, 49, 56
Reversible patches, 82
Ribbon Facing, 14
Rice, Nancy Nix-, 1, 3
Round Pocket With Button, 37
Ruffle, 17
Saddle Bag Pockets, 79
Saddle Bag With Flap, 79
Safari jackets, 61
Seam tape hems, 101
Self-Lined Pocket With Bound Edge, 32
Serged hems, 101
Serger finish, 3
Setting the pocket, 4, 102
Sew-in interfacings, 95, 107
Shaped Band, Pleated Pocket With, 70
Shaping the pocket, 106
Shirt Method, hem finish, 3
Smith, Shirley, 57
Special fabrics, 107
Square corners, 35
Square Inside-Stitched Pocket, 42
Squared corner with binding, 33
Squared corners, pressing, 3
Standards for patch pockets, *ix*
Stripes, 15, 76
    Tucked, 56
Sweater knits, 108
Tailor tacks, 93
Template, 104, 105
Thread tracing, 24, 93
Toile, *x*
Topstitched hems, 102
Topstitched pockets, 104
Topstitching, 31, 89, 102
    Invisible, 34
Tracing wheel, 93
Trenched application for interfacing, 96
Tuck strip, 8, 51
Tuck Terminology, 50
Tucked Hem, 8
Tucked Stripes, 56
Tucks, 49
    Overlapping, 53
    Reverse, 56
Turn-of-the-cloth, 88
Turned-and-stitched hems, 101
Underlay, 60
    Separate, 63
Underlining, 98
Unlined One-Piece Bellows Pocket, 72
Unlined Pocket With a Tucked Hem, 8
Unlined Pocket With Band, 10
Unlined Pocket With Cut-on Cuff, 45
Unlined Pocket With One-Piece Cuff, 47
Unlined Pocket With Ribbon Facing, 14
Unlined pockets, 1+
Utilitarian Edge-to-Edge Lining, 28, 29
Utilitarian pocket, 18
Whittemore, Pat, 4, 104
Wolfe, Mary Gorgen, 92
Zieman, Nancy, 36
Zigzagged hems, 101

Other Books Available From Chilton

Robbie Fanning, Series Editor

Contemporary Quilting Series

Appliqué the Ann Boyce Way, by Ann Boyce
Contemporary Quilting Techniques, by Pat Cairns
Fast Patch, by Anita Hallock
Fourteen Easy Baby Quilts, by Margaret Dittman
Machine-Quilted Jackets, Vests, and Coats, by Nancy Moore
Pictorial Quilts, by Carolyn Hall
Precision-Pieced Quilts Using the Foundation Method, by Jane Hall and Dixie Haywood
Quick Quilted Home Decor With Your Sewing Machine, by Jackie Dodson
The Quilter's Guide to Rotary Cutting, by Donna Poster
Quilts by the Slice, by Beckie Olson
Scrap Quilts Using Fast Patch, by Anita Hallock
Speed-Cut Quilts, by Donna Poster
Super Simple Quilts, by Kathleen Eaton
Teach Yourself Machine Piecing and Quilting, by Debra Wagner
Three-Dimensional Appliqué, by Jodie Davis

Creative Machine Arts Series

ABCs of Serging, by Tammy Young and Lori Bottom
The Button Lover's Book, by Marilyn Green
Claire Shaeffer's Fabric Sewing Guide
The Complete Book of Machine Embroidery, by Robbie and Tony Fanning
Creative Nurseries Illustrated, by Debra Terry and Juli Plooster
Creative Serging Illustrated, The New, by Pati Palmer, Gail Brown, and Sue Green
Distinctive Serger Gifts and Crafts, by Naomi Baker and Tammy Young
The Fabric Lover's Scrapbook, by Margaret Dittman
Friendship Quilts by Hand and Machine, by Carolyn Vosburg Hall
Gifts Galore, by Jane Warnick and Jackie Dodson
How to Make Soft Jewelry, by Jackie Dodson
Innovative Serging, by Gail Brown and Tammy Young
Innovative Sewing, by Gail Brown and Tammy Young
Owner's Guide to Sewing Machines, Sergers, and Knitting Machines, by Gale Grigg Hazen
Petite Pizzazz, by Barb Griffin
Putting on the Glitz, by Sandra L. Hatch and Ann Boyce
Second Stitches, by Susan D. Parker
Serge a Simple Project, by Tammy Young and Naomi Baker
Serged Garments in Minutes, by Tammy Young and Naomi Baker
Sew Sensational Gifts, by Naomi Baker and Tammy Young
Sew, Serge, Press, by Jan Saunders
Sewing and Collecting Vintage Fashions, by Eileen MacIntosh
Simply Serge Any Fabric, by Naomi Baker and Tammy Young
Soft Gardens, by Yvonne Perez-Collins
Twenty Easy Machine-Made Rugs, by Jackie Dodson

Open Chain Books

Gail Brown's All-New Instant Interiors, by Gail Brown
Jane Asher's Costume Book, by Gail Brown
Learn Bearmaking, by Judi Maddigan
Quick Napkin Creations, by Gail Brown
Sew Any Patch Pocket, by Claire Shaeffer
Singer Instructions for Art Embroidery and Lace Work
Soft Toys for Babies, by Judi Maddigan

Crafts Kaleidoscope

Fabric Painting Made Easy, by Nancy Ward
How to Make Cloth Books for Children, by Anne Pellowski
Quick and Easy Ways With Ribbon, by Ceci Johnson
Too Hot to Handle?/Potholders and How to Make Them, by Doris Hoover

StarWear

Embellishments, by Linda Fry Kenzle
Sweatshirts With Style, by Mary Mulari

Know Your Sewing Machine Series, by Jackie Dodson

Know Your Bernina, second edition
Know Your Brother, with Jane Warnick
Know Your Elna, with Carol Ahles
Know Your New Home, with Judi Cull and Vicki Lynn Hastings
Know Your Pfaff, with Audrey Griese
Know Your Sewing Machine
Know Your Singer
Know Your Viking, with Jan Saunders
Know Your White, with Jan Saunders

Know Your Serger Series, by Tammy Young and Naomi Baker

Know Your baby lock
Know Your Pfaff Hobbylock
Know Your Serger
Know Your White Superlock

Teach Yourself to Sew Better Series, by Jan Saunders

A Step-by-Step Guide to Your Bernina
A Step-by-Step Guide to Your New Home
A Step-by-Step Guide to Your Sewing Machine
A Step-by-Step Guide to Your Viking